The Instructional Leader's Guide to Informal Classroom Observations

Sally J. Zepeda

EYE ON EDUCATION

6 DEPOT WAY WEST, SUITE 106

LARCHMONT, NY 10538

(914) 833–0551

(914) 833–0761 fax

www.eyeoneducation.com

Library of Congress Cataloging-in-Publication Data

Zepeda, Sally J., 1956-
The instructional leader's guide to informal classroom observations / Sally J. Zepeda.
      p. cm.
   ISBN 1-59667-010-X
  1. Observation (Educational method) 2. School principals—United States. 3. Teacher-principal relationships—United States. 4. School supervision—United States. I. Title.
  LB1731.6.Z46 2005
  371.2'03—dc22

                                   2005016662

10 9 8 7 6 5 4 3 2

Editorial and production services provided by
Richard H. Adin Freelance Editorial Services
52 Oakwood Blvd., Poughkeepsie, NY 12603-4112
(845-471-3566)

Also Available from EYE ON EDUCATION

The Principal as Instructional Leader:
A Handbook for Supervisors
Sally J. Zepeda

Standards for Instructional Supervision:
Enhancing Teaching and Learning
Edited by Stephen P. Gordon

Instructional Leadership for School Improvement
Sally J. Zepeda

Instructional Supervision: Applying Tools and Concepts
Sally J. Zepeda

Supervision Across the Content Areas
Sally J. Zepeda and R. Stewart Mayers

The Call to Teacher Leadership
Sally J. Zepeda, R. Stewart Mayers, & Brad N. Benson

Staff Development:
Practices That Promote Leadership in Learning Communities
Sally J. Zepeda

What Great Principals Do Differently:
5 Things That Matter Most
Todd Whitaker

What Great Teachers Do Differently:
14 Things That Matter Most
Todd Whitaker

101 "Answers" for New Teachers and Their Mentors:
Effective Teaching Tips for Daily Classroom Use
Annette L. Breaux

Data Analysis for Continuous School Improvement,
Second Edition
Victoria L. Bernhardt

What Successful Principals Do!
169 Tips for Principals
Franzy Fleck

Great Quotes for Great Educators
Todd Whitaker and Dale Lumpa

BRAVO Principal!
Sandra Harris

**Stepping Outside Your Comfort Zone:
Lessons for School Leaders**
Nelson Beaudoin

**Dealing with Difficult Teachers,
Second Edition**
Todd Whitaker

**Dealing with Difficult Parents
(And with Parents in Difficult Situations)**
Todd Whitaker and Douglas Fiore

**Motivating & Inspiring Teachers
The Educational Leader's Guide for Building Staff Morale**
Todd Whitaker, Beth Whitaker, and Dale Lumpa

**The ISLLC Standards in Action:
A Principal's Handbook**
Carol Engler

**Harnessing the Power of Resistance:
A Guide for Educators**
Jared Scherz

**Administrator's Guide to School Community Relations,
Second Ed.**
George E. Pawlas

**School Leader Internship: Developing, Monitoring,
and Evaluating Your Leadership Experience**
Martin, Wright, Danzig, Flanary and Brown

**Handbook on Teacher Evaluation:
Assessing and Improving Performance**
James Stronge & Pamela Tucker

About the Author

Sally J. Zepeda served as a high school teacher, department chair, assistant principal, principal, and director of special programs before entering higher education. She is an associate professor and graduate coordinator in the Department of Lifelong Education, Administration, and Policy in the Program of Educational Administration and Policy at the University of Georgia, where she teaches courses in instructional supervision, professional development, teacher evaluation, and school improvement.

Sally has written widely about instructional leadership and the supervision and evaluation of teaching. In 2004, she edited a special issue of the *NASSP Bulletin* on instructional supervision for the National Association of Secondary School Principals.

Sally's 10 books include *Supervision Across the Content Areas* (with R. Stewart Mayers); *Instructional Leadership for School Improvement*; *The Principal as Instructional Leader: A Handbook for Supervisors*; *Instructional Supervision: Applying Tools and Concepts*; *The Call to Teacher Leadership* (with R. Stewart Mayers and Brad Benson); *Staff Development: Practices That Promote Leadership in Learning Communities*; *Hands-on Leadership Tools for Principals* (with Raymond Calabrese and Gary Short); *The Reflective Supervisor: A Practical Guide for Educators* (with Raymond Calabrese); *Special Programs in Regular Schools: Historical Foundations, Standards, and Contemporary Issues* (with Michael Langenbach); and *Supervision and Staff Development in the Block* (with R. Stewart Mayers).

Acknowledgements

The professionals who reviewed this manuscript shared their perspectives selflessly, making this book stronger because of their insights. I am indebted to these professionals—Richard A. Flanary, Director of NASSP's Department of Professional Development Services; Laura McCullough, Director of Instructional Services, Waynesboro School District, Virginia, and Todd Wiedemann, Principal, Berrien Springs High School, Michigan.

There are always people who work behind the scenes while a book is being written. A special acknowledgement goes to Marc Ginsberg, a graduate assistant in the Department of Lifelong Education, Administration, and Policy at the University of Georgia. Marc provided invaluable assistance proofreading and helping me to meet deadlines. Bob Sickles challenged and encouraged me to write this book after I "gritched" about the lost art of informal classroom observation as it was envisioned many years ago. Amy Barrett provided invaluable editorial assistance. Perhaps no one worked behind the scenes more than Richard Adin, who provided expert guidance on the final layout and design of this book. What a great team!

Classroom Observation Tools

Table of Contents

1

Readying for Informal Classroom Observations

In This Chapter...

- ♦ Principals make the commitment to get out and about
- ♦ Principals know their people
- ♦ Principals assess the context of supervision and their own beliefs
- ♦ Principals develop the leadership skills of the administrative team
- ♦ Principals develop practices to track the observation efforts of the administrative team

A resounding finding in the literature of the accountability movement is that teacher quality improves student learning. If this premise is true, then the assessment of teaching *in classrooms* needs to become the first step toward improving instruction and assisting teachers to examine their practices. Assisting teachers begins at the place where instruction occurs—in the classroom. Principals and other school leaders are urged to remember that, like students, teachers need opportunities to grow, develop, and learn.

What Is This Book About?

This book focuses on assisting the principal (and others) as he or she works with teachers in formative ways, primarily through informal classroom observations. To make informal classroom observations a priority, principals must frame their work habits and daily routines around dropping by classrooms and then following up by providing teachers with feedback and opportunities for reflection and inquiry. This book is written for the principal who wants to be viewed by teachers as a support for the instructional program. Assistant principals, department chairs, lead teachers, teacher leaders, and others can enhance the instructional program by developing a better understanding of informal classroom observations. This book provides a series of classroom observation tools to help frame the informal classroom observation and follow-up discussion with teachers.

Why Informal Classroom Observations Are Important

Informal classroom observation is a way to get instructional supervision and teacher evaluation out of the main office. Teachers need feedback more than once or twice a year. Informal classroom observations provide valuable opportunities for more frequent interaction between the supervisor and the teacher. Informal classroom observations can provide opportunities to extend the talk about teaching if the principal carves out enough time after an informal classroom observation to engage teachers in a discussion of their instructional practices.

Recently, informal classroom observations have become vogue with principals who are learning the art and science of the "three-minute walk-through" advocated by the research, practice, and work of Downey, Steffy, English, Frase, and Poston (2004). The value of the three-minute walk-through as an approach is acknowledged as a practice. This book, however, offers a different view of informal classroom observations. Namely, the informal classroom observation should be extended to more than three minutes to achieve its purposes—working with teachers in ways that are more meaningful. A three-minute walk-through is simply not enough time to capture a sustained picture of teaching and learning, and that is why this book advocates a more enlarged view of the informal classroom observation. In general, teachers want context-specific information about their teaching, and data observed in the window of a 15- to 20-minute observation can provide such opportunities for specific feedback, discussion, and reflection.

Teaching and Learning to Teach Are Complex

Part of the process of learning to teach occurs in the overall school context and in the varying contexts of classrooms where instruction unfolds in the presence of children. Learning to teach is mediated through such variables as experience, preparation route (traditional or alternative certification), the professional development opportunities in which teachers engage, and so on.

Teachers learn to teach on the job through their experiences as they plan for instruction and interact with their students. When teachers have the opportunity to talk about teaching, to share their insights with someone else, and to reflect on what occurs in the classroom, their learning increases. This type of job-embedded learning is enhanced through the efforts of the observant principal, who facilitates opportunities for teachers to reflect and refine their practices through sustained feedback based on data from informal classroom observations.

Principals Make the Commitment to Get Out and About

The overall intent of instructional supervision is teacher growth and development. Effective supervisors do not wait to be invited into classrooms; they find opportunities for informal visits in addition to the more formal, mandated classroom observations tied to evaluation. They constantly scan the learning environment for ways to help teachers improve on their talents.

Principals who find time to drop by classrooms seek and value opportunities to connect with their teachers, and they have a sincere desire to see teachers succeed as they face classroom challenges. Based on what principals observe in classrooms over time, they are able to do the following:

◆ Extend the talk about teaching and learning.

◆ Make purposeful efforts to promote whole-school involvement by sharing what others has learned.

◆ Involve others in conducting informal classroom observations, including members of the administrative team, department chairs, and teachers.

◆ Get creative about sharing what has been learned through faculty newsletters, electronic mailing lists, and video clips with promising teaching practices as an entire team.

◆ Embed learning and professional development opportunities based on the reality of the school's context.

With a commitment to making informal classroom observations a part of the workday, these goals are achievable. The principal must wrap his or her thinking around the context of the school and the characteristics of the teachers in the building and then carve out time in an already busy and hectic workday. Effective leaders "know their people."

Principals Know Their People

Effective leaders do their homework up front, even before conducting their first informal classroom observation. These leaders know their people, in part, because they do several things:

- Assess the characteristics of teachers.
- Recognize teachers' career stages.
- Assess teachers' willingness to learn.
- Know, honor, and respect the adult learner.

Assessing the Characteristics of Teachers

Tool 1 will assist you in broadly profiling any given faculty. By gathering statistical information about a school's faculty, the principal can begin to reflect about teachers' learning needs. It might be useful to have a faculty roster and, if it is available, a seniority list (typically available from the district office) to help track and tally information.

Tool 1 Assessing the Broad Characteristics of a Faculty

1. Number of teachers = *103*   Male = *42* Female = *61*

2. For each teacher, tally the number of years in teaching.
   Total number of years of experience = *900*
   Average years of faculty experience = *9*

3. Number of teachers whose experience falls within the following service ranges:

   a. 1–3 years = *23*

   b. 4–7 years = *45*

   c. 8–11 years = *0*

   d. 12–15 years = *15*

   e. 16–19 years = *0*

   f. 20+ years = *20*

4. Number of first-year teachers = *11*
   Number of teachers who will retire at the end of the year = *19*

5. Wildcards:
   First-year teachers with experience = *0*
   Alternatively certified teachers = *5*
   Teachers returning to work after an extended leave = *2*
   Other = *0*

6. What overall patterns do you notice?
   About 20% of these teachers have three or fewer years of experience.
   About half of the teachers are at the midpoint of their careers.
   About 20% of the teachers are in the wind-down stage of their careers.
   About 18% of the teachers are going to retire; there will more than likely be an influx of less experienced teachers hired the following year.

To extend the contextual information about the broad characteristics of teachers in the building, the principal next examines teacher career stages.

Recognizing Teachers' Career Stages

Regardless of experience, position, grade level, or subject area, learning to teach is a process that continues throughout one's career, and this is why instructional supervision is important. As adults, teachers have learning needs that shift over time, signaling inexact stages of development. At one time, most teachers entered the profession immediately following a four-year preparation program. Now, many teachers enter the profession through alternative certification routes. Suffice it to say, knowledge about teachers' career stages is important if principals are going to work more effectively to improve instructional support through the informal classroom observation process.

Figure 1.1 provides an inexact but useful way of thinking about teachers' career stages. The types of professional supports that teachers need at the beginning of their careers are very different from those needed by teachers who are further along in their careers.

Figure 1.1 Teachers' Career Stages and Developmental Needs

Stage	Name	Years in Field (approximate)	Developmental Theory and Needs
1	Preservice	0	Training and preparation for a profession
2	Induction	1–2	Survival stage: Seeks safety and desires to learn the day-to-day operations of the school and the complexities of facing new situations in the classroom
3	Competency	3–5	Confidence in work mounts, as does understanding of the multifaceted role of teaching
4	Enthusiasm	5–8	Actively seeks professional development and other opportunities; high job satisfaction
5	Career frustration	Varies	Teacher burnout
6	Stability	Varies	Complacency; innovation is low
7	Career wind down	Varies	Coasts on past laurels and status; little effort
8	Career exit	Varies	End of teaching career

Adapted from Burden (1982); Burke, Christensen, & Fessler (1984); Christensen, Burke, Fessler, & Hagstrom (1983); Feiman & Floden (1980); Huberman, 1993; Katz, 1972.

Through an educator's career span, Burden (1982, pp. 1–2) found that many changes occur in the following areas:

◆ job skills, knowledge, and behaviors—in areas such as teaching methods, discipline strategies, and curriculum planning

◆ attitudes and outlooks—in areas such as images of teaching, professional confidence and maturity, and willingness to try new teaching methods and concerns

◆ job events—in areas such as changes in grade level, school, or district; involvement in additional professional responsibilities; and age of entry and retirement

Given this range, it is logical for principals to use informal classroom observation as a tool to assist teachers with the uncertainties they face as a result of these changes. These changes also can affect teachers' willingness to learn.

Assessing Teachers' Willingness to Learn

People learn at their own pace, and workplace conditions, such as the relationship between administration and teachers and the norms of collegiality, affect learning. Learning can neither be mandated nor imposed. Adults respond to learning opportunities differently. Principals can be more effective if they know their teachers as "learners," just as effective teachers know when to shift instruction and learning activities to meet the individual and collective needs of students in the classroom. From this perspective, the principal is encouraged to view the school as a classroom in which all members are engaged in learning individually and collectively. The principal is able to assess current practices by examining the following:

◆ *Learning:* Do teachers seek out learning opportunities offered at the site, district, or externally (graduate school, local and national conferences, and workshops)?

◆ *Sharing:* Do teachers share their knowledge and expertise with other teachers? Do teachers meet to share what they have learned in professional development activities?

◆ *Reflecting and discussing:* Do teachers openly discuss what they have learned about their own teaching practices?

◆ *Examining the talk over time:* Are discussions held over sustained periods? One-time discussions do little to promote professional growth; continual discussion about progress and setbacks promotes personal and professional development.

◆ *Reading the word:* Are books, professional journals, and technology used as resources? Are these resources readily available and shared?

After examining these conditions, principals can further ready for conducting informal classroom observations by understanding teachers as adult learners.

Knowing, Honoring, and Respecting the Adult Learner

Although this book is limited in its coverage of the principles of adult learning, there are several assumptions about adult learning that serve as a baseline for helping principals work more effectively with teachers.

The principal who promotes adult development strives to make learning experiences

- ◆ self-directed, with the learner at the center of all activities;
- ◆ collaborative and promote trust, reflection, and open exchanges;
- ◆ ongoing and sustained (Brookfield, 1986; Knowles, 1980).

Getting out of the office and entering the classroom to observe teachers is an important way to honor teachers' work and to help them to grow as adult learners. By committing time and effort, the principal who becomes a welcome guest in the classroom does so not by directing or being critical of the teacher, but by forming a partnership with the teacher. The value of the principal getting out and about lies in the opportunity to provide teachers with occasions to reflect on their classroom practices through the objective data collected in informal observations. The power of the feedback and dialogue that results from such learning opportunities will be examined in later chapters.

Principals Assess the Context of Supervision and Their Own Beliefs

Teachers want accessible, visible principals, but they do not want simple, open- door policies or mobile principals in the halls during passing periods. Teachers want principals to visit them in their classrooms, and they desire constructive feedback. Assessment of the context of supervision includes understanding the history of supervision and evaluation, knowing the intent and purpose of supervision and evaluation, and reflecting on the interactions between teachers and the principal (past and present). These factors shape the environment in which supervision evolves as a proactive process.

To create the conditions for effective informal classroom observations, the principal needs to reflect on the nature of the interactions that surround supervisory practices. The principal can assess the nature of prior classroom observations by asking, answering, and then reflecting on the meanings that his or her responses hold for the following questions:

- ◆ Are teachers used to seeing me and other administrators in their classrooms beyond the mandated classroom observations used to evaluate?

- Do I merely report what I observe?
- Do I try to link other activities, such as professional development, to the supervisory process?
- Are post-observation conferences conducted in a timely manner?
- Where are pre- and post-observation conferences conducted? (In the teacher's classroom? The main office?)

Learning and refining existing supervisory skills are ongoing practices that continually evolve as one gains experience and nurtures working relationships with teachers.

The principal often works with other site administrators and teacher leaders who should be a part of the supervisory efforts. The principal is encouraged to spend time nurturing administrative team members.

Principals Develop the Leadership Skills of the Administrative Team

There is no substitute for the principal's visible presence in classrooms; however, there is a need for the administrative team to be engaged in the work of informal classroom observations. This involvement will multiply efforts, and, by including members of the administrative team in the work of informal classroom observations, the principal is in a position to create important conditions to do the following:

- promote dialogue
- affirm teachers' strengths
- assist teachers in identifying areas of instruction to bolster
- target areas for professional development
- encourage reflection

Given the relative size of many schools, it is almost impossible to expect the principal to stand alone, conducting all informal classroom observations. First, however, members of the administrative team need to be informed and prepared to take on this responsibility. A solid beginning point is to understand the beliefs, values, and assumptions that the administrative team hold regarding teaching, learning, and the efforts needed to support teachers through informal classroom observations. These understandings are important because an administrative team that operates with similar beliefs, values, and assumptions sends a unified and powerful message to teachers—including support for their efforts to become more effective in the classroom.

As the leader, the principal is encouraged to set aside time for sustained discussion so that administrative team members can collectively explore their responses to the following open-ended statements:

- As a team, we plan for…
- As a team, we monitor…
- As a team, we model…
- As a team, we recognize and celebrate…
- As a team, we will are willing to confront…
- As a team, we believe effective teachers…
- As a team, we believe an effective classroom is one in which…
- As a team, we believe teachers grow professionally…
- As a team, we support teaching and learning by…

Without such introspection, the school's administrative team will not be synchronized to work alongside the principal to meet the needs of teachers. An administrative team that works together can do the following:

- build a unified vision for supervision and professional development
- create a healthy learning culture
- serve as valuable resources to teachers meeting their needs
- coordinate and provide appropriate learning opportunities based on these needs
- grow as professionals from their work in the school

Making informal classroom observations an administrative priority takes concerted effort on the part of the principal and the administrative team. It takes time to make informal classroom observations a habit of mind and practice. Such a commitment is really a commitment to the overall improvement of the instructional program that focuses on the efforts of teachers but is dependent, in part, on the following abilities of the administrative team:

- *Redefine relationships with each other and with teachers.* This redefining process begins with the principal flattening the hierarchical structures within leadership teams (e.g., principal, associate principal, assistant principal, deans, instructional deans, department chairs, lead teachers, and grade-level coordinators).
- *Share responsibility for learning.* All team members need to assume an active role in providing learning opportunities for themselves as they work with teachers.

◆ *Create an atmosphere of interdependence.* Each member of the team needs to feel a sense of belonging, contributing to individual and collective learning opportunities while working alongside fellow administrative team members and teachers.

◆ *Make time for professional development.* Time is often cited as the main reason why principals and other members of the administrative team cannot function as instructional leaders. Consider your reaction if a teacher indicated that he or she did not have time to make it to class or correct student work.

◆ *Develop a plan for professional development, with teacher needs guiding the process.* No plan, if it is not grounded in the needs of its learners, will yield significant results.

◆ *Rotate responsibilities.* Rotation of specific duties and responsibilities associated with professional development can help to get all members of the administrative team on the same proverbial page. This rotation also can assist with breaking down barriers between people within the organization while supporting the development of skills and expertise for all team members.

◆ *Link schoolwide initiatives.* The coordination of school initiatives will reduce unnecessary duplication of programs and provide resources to support initiatives.

Principals Develop Practices to Track the Observation Efforts of the Administrative Team

Informal observations should be tracked. Tool 2 (see page 13) provides an example of how principals can track the informal classroom observations made by administrative team members.

By reviewing the record of formal and informal classroom observations, principals can determine whether any teachers were missed, whether observations were spread evenly throughout a portion of the school year or the day (indicated by the period or time of the observation), what follow-up topics were discussed, and when the post-observation conferences occurred. Principals also can look for patterns. For example, in Tool 2, Marlowe did not observe Baker at all for four months, and there was a delay in the follow-up; Linton balanced informal and informal observations, and Burton did not engage Schmidt in any follow-up to the informal classroom observations. The principal should interpret these patterns in the context of the school and the characteristics of the teachers being supervised.

Tool 2 Tracking Informal Observations

Teacher	Observer	Informal Observations	Date of Follow-up	Formal Observations	Period(s)/ Time(s)	Follow-up Topics
Adams	Schmidt	9/01/2005 11/07/2005	9/02/2005 11/10/2005	10/05/2005	1 (8:15–8:30) 5 (11:10–11:20)	Cooperative learning grouping
Baker	Marlowe	11/08/2005	11/20/2005	3/20/2005	1 (8:15–8:25) 1 (8:15–8:25)	Instructional pacing
Beatty	Linton	9/05/2005 9/08/2005 10/18/2005 1/12/2006	9/06/2005 9/08/2005 10/20/2005 1/14/2006	0/07/2005 10/14/2005 11/02/2005 12/05/2005	1 (8:30–8:45) 3 (10:10–10:25) 1 (8:15–8:25) 6 (1:05–1:15)	Classroom management; beginning- and end-of-period procedures
Burton	Schmidt	9/07/2005 11/20/2005	None None	10/31/2005	1 (8:00–8:15) 8 (2:15–2:30)	Classroom management

Looking Ahead...

The next chapter details the intent of informal classroom observations, the premise behind informal classroom observations, and some basic guidelines to consider.

2

Framing Informal Classroom Observations

In This Chapter...

- ◆ The intents of teacher observation and instructional supervision
- ◆ Informal classroom observations
- ◆ Guidelines for informal classroom observations

To be enduring, a supervisory program that includes informal classroom observations that go beyond hit and miss requires an understanding of the intents of teacher observation and supervision. Informal classroom observations need to be based on guidelines to bolster teacher learning and development, and they should not be viewed or conducted as a "drive-through" in which a principal blitzes in and out of the classroom without offering some type of feedback. The drive-through approach just does not give the principal enough time to capture the events of the classroom, to collect data that are stable, or to provide enough hooks to engage the teacher in reflective dialogue.

The Intents of Teacher Observation
and Instructional Supervision

Observing teachers in action is the primary way of assessing teaching. Through formal and informal classroom observations, principals gain insights into classroom practices: instructional strategies, learning activities (including performance assessments), the taught curriculum, and the types of teacher and student interactions that evolve throughout the course of instruction. Effective classroom observations support the overall instructional program and the teachers who deliver it. Classroom observations also signal to teachers that the principal cares about them and the work they do. The principal's classroom presence promotes a healthy climate and creates conditions for the ongoing discussion, reflection, and refinement of practices.

Both Teachers and Principals Benefit from Classroom Observations

Classroom observations, whether they are formal or informal, provide opportunities for both the principal and the teacher to develop a broader range of understanding of the complexities of teaching and learning. For this range of understanding to emerge, classroom observations must occur over time with sustained attention to the processes used to observe teachers (observation tools are examined in Chapter 4). Classroom observations provide opportunities *for teachers* to do the following:

- learn more about their teaching through the principal's support and presence and to extend talk about teaching and reduce feelings of isolation
- examine what works well and which areas of instruction or classroom management could be enhanced by modifying practice
- be affirmed for their instructional efforts
- gauge short- and long-term efforts by examining objective data collected over a sustained period of time

For principals, there are benefits and opportunities as well. Principals benefit from informal observations because they

- learn more about teaching and learning
- share alternative strategies observed in other classrooms with teachers
- frame professional development opportunities for teachers across grade levels and subject areas

- have a deeper understanding of the complexities of the classroom and how teachers handle these complexities
- lend assistance to teachers who have needs
- have more than snapshot views of teachers
- enhance the supervisory and evaluation plan at the site

The intents of supervision are to improve teaching and to lend assistance to teachers as they move throughout their careers. To this end, supervision is a proactive, ongoing set of processes and procedures.

Informal Classroom Observations

Every school system has processes in place for formal teacher evaluations that are based on state statutes regarding evaluation, union agreements, and other context-specific factors that make each school system unique. It is wise to know systemwide policies and procedures, along with the history of supervision at the site. Notwithstanding, the way that informal observations are conducted will dictate teachers' willingness to embrace informal observation as an ongoing component of professional learning.

Management by Wandering Around

Informal classroom observation has evolved in the literature and in practice. Recently, there has been resurgence in attention to informal classroom observation. The popularity of informal classroom observation can be tied to the *management by wandering around* (MBWA) movement, which was popularized by Peters and Waterman (1982) in their book *In Search of Excellence: Lessons From America's Best Run Companies*.

Executives who embraced MBWA promoted informal communication and personal involvement with employees by getting out of the office. Through this accessibility and visibility, executives were able to ensure accountability and affirm the work of employees. The practice of informal classroom observations also embraces getting supervision and evaluation out of the main office, situating principals as active participants in the instructional lives of their teachers by promoting visibility and accessibility.

Walking-Around Supervision and Short Visits

In the supervision and teacher evaluation literature, informal classroom observations have been tied to both formative and summative evaluation practices. Manning (1988) asserted that information about teachers gleaned from "walking-around supervision" and "short visits" should be included as summative samplings in the overall evaluation of teaching. Although the two are similar, Manning makes a sharp distinction between walking-around supervision and short visits. Walking-around supervision promotes the visibility of the principal but primarily "in the halls...before and after the first bell in the morning, and immediately before the dismissal bell in the afternoon" (p. 145) and in the lunchrooms. During these and other times, the principal takes in information about instruction and plans short visits if there is a need (e.g., a teacher who is having difficulties with classroom management or a teacher who is regarded as having an exemplary instructional method). According to Manning, short visits last longer, "less than a full class period." Also, "it is important to always follow up a short visit with a brief conference," especially "if a problem is noted, the principal can discuss this...and plan for a additional evaluation" (p. 146).

Catch Teachers in the Act of Teaching

The principal does *not* conduct informal classroom visitations to catch the teacher off guard or by surprise or to interrupt classroom activities. Informal classroom observations allow principals to affirm what teachers are doing right by encouraging them to keep up the momentum. Moreover, informal observations allow the principal and teacher to celebrate successes in teaching and student learning.

Informal observations are one way instructional supervisors can get to know their teachers. By observing teacher's work *in their classrooms*, principals can exert informed effort and energy to assist teachers beyond formally scheduled observations. Informal observations provide opportunities for supervisors to do the following:

- ◆ motivate teachers
- ◆ monitor instruction
- ◆ be accessible and provide support
- ◆ keep informed about instruction in the school (Blase & Blase, 1998, pp. 108–109)

An Observation by Any Other Name

Sometimes referred to as *pop-ins, walk-ins,* or *drop-ins,* informal classroom observations have the following characteristics:

- ◆ They are brief, lasting approximately 15 to 20 minutes (perhaps longer).
- ◆ They can occur at the beginning, middle, or end of a period.
- ◆ They can occur at any time during the school day.

◆ They focus on a variety of aspects, including instruction, use of time, classroom management, transitions between learning activities, or the clarity of instructions.

Informal classroom observation is a strategy for getting into classrooms, with the intent to focus on teaching, learning, and the interactions between teachers and students as the events of instruction unfold.

Informal observations are not intended to supplant formal ones; they do not include a pre-observation conference. Too often, informal classroom observations forgo post-observation conferences. The principal is reminded that the value of the informal observation, which culminates with an opportunity to talk with teachers, is that principals can strengthen their relationships with teachers by communicating *something* about what was observed. In fact, a majority of informal observations should include some type of follow-up conversation about teaching and learning. Chapter 4 details tools that can be used to chronicle what is observed during informal classroom observations, and Chapter 5 offers techniques for communicating what is observed, along with strategies to assist teachers in reflecting on their practices.

Three Minutes Is Not Enough

The interest in informal classroom observations was piqued by the Downey Informal Observation method, in which principals spend three to five minutes observing a classroom (Downey, Steffy, English, Frase, & Poston, 2005). Although that method will certainly get supervision out of the main office, the principal is encouraged to spend more than three to five minutes in the classroom during an informal observation to have a meaningful experience. The egg-timer approach to classroom observation of this duration is a "blitz" in which the observation's brevity minimizes data collection. It would be preferable to conduct fewer but longer informal observations on a daily basis to connect with teachers and to derive a more accurate sense of the classroom activities observed.

The principal's daily struggle is to find time for mandatory formal classroom observations and informal classroom visits. Although no clear-cut solution to this problem applies across all school systems, many principals have found creative ways to make the most of their available human resources and to provide a supervisory program centered on teachers' needs. A commitment to being more visible to teachers will be strengthened by the impact that classroom visitations can have on strengthening the instructional program; the dividend is movement toward high-quality learning for the teachers who are entrusted to educate children.

Guidelines for Informal Classroom Observations

The following guidelines for informal classroom observations are offered as a starting point for framing this important work.

Guidelines for Informal Classroom Observations

Informally observe all teachers

All teachers can benefit from informal classroom observation. Refrain from "overobserving" teachers (e.g., only teachers who are having difficulty, beginning teachers, teachers who teach subject areas that are heavily tested). Informal classroom observation should last between 15 and 20 minutes; therefore, conduct only as many observations in a day as you can follow up on either the same day as the observation or the very next day. Teachers need and deserve some type of feedback that is immediate.

Informally observe as often as you can

The principal's presence in classrooms sends a positive message to teachers: The principal cares. Including informal classroom observation as a schoolwide initiative requires consistency and frequency. Become opportunistic in finding time in the day to observe teachers, and vary the time of the day in which you observe teachers. What occurs in the morning is much different than what occurs in the afternoon.

Watch, listen, and write, but focus on one or two areas

Although there is no predetermined focus established during a pre-observation conference, find a focus based on the instruction, events, or discussions that are occurring in the classroom. Avoid having a predetermined focus in which teachers know how to teach to the hot spot of the observer. For example, if the principal is a proponent of cooperative learning, teachers might be tempted to transition to cooperative learning activities once the principal enters the room.

Given that informal observations are relatively brief (15–20 minutes) compared to an extended classroom observation (30–45 minutes), data from a single focus will make for richer conversation during follow-up discussion.

Guidelines for Informal Classroom Observations

Have fun

Check your demeanor—let your body language and facial expressions communicate that you are enjoying the time in the classroom. A principal's demeanor sends strong messages—either the principal enjoys being out and about, or the principal grudgingly engages in informal classroom observations. Think about how you want teachers and students to view you.

Catch them in the act of doing something right and applaud efforts

Look for victories rather than failures and applaud them. Work to create an ethos of sharing. Teachers who are especially adept at a strategy or technique need time and opportunities for sharing their expertise with others. For example, a certain amount of time at weekly or monthly faculty meetings could be set aside for teachers to share insights or techniques with one another.

Make the time to follow up

Follow-up communication to informal classroom observation is a critical component. Through conversations and reflection, teachers better understand the complexities of their work. Feedback and dialogue form the cornerstone of all supervisory activities.

Follow up with resources

After feedback, the effective principal follows up with resources that teachers need to refine practice. The principal's efforts to return for a follow-up informal observation might be a resource to provide.

Take informal observations invitational

Encourage teachers to invite you to observe them. Teachers who are experimenting with unique or novel instructional approaches or whose students are making presentations would welcome the opportunity for the principal to be present.

Adapted from FutureCents (2005).

Looking Ahead...

The next chapter explores the intents of data collection and some broad techniques to consider before exploring and applying the classroom observation tools presented in Chapter 4.

3

Understanding Data Collection Techniques and Approaches

In This Chapter...

- ◆ Intents of data collection
- ◆ Types of data and data-collection techniques

Fertile data can be gleaned from an informal classroom observation lasting between 15 and 20 minutes. More than merely watching during an informal observation, the principal collects stable and useful data. Accurate and bias-free data will further assist teachers in making sense of their teaching. The intents of data collection and data-collection techniques are examined in this chapter, and in Chapter 4, the data-collection tools used during classroom observations will be applied.

Intents of Data Collection

The adage "less is more" is worth exploring given that an informal classroom observation lasts a relatively short time. Brevity, coupled with the fast-paced nature of activities in a classroom, dictates that the principal focus on less to provide a more detailed and richer portrayal of what occurred. Many types of data can be collected during an informal classroom observation. Consider the possibilities:

- engagement of the learner through the content
- instructional methods used to deliver the content
- types of activities that engage learners
- resources used to enhance learning experiences
- types of assessments used to make judgments about learning

These areas and more are important to teaching and learning, and all deserve attention. According to McGreal (1988, pp. 21–22), there are four intents of data collection that should drive the observation and the tools used to collect data.

1. The reliability and usefulness of classroom observation is related to the amount and types of information that supervisors have prior to the observation.

2. The narrower the focus that supervisors use in observing classrooms, the more likely they will be to describe the events related to that focus.

3. The impact of observational data is related to the way the data are recorded during the observation.

4. The impact of observational data on supervisor–teacher relationships is related to the way feedback is presented to the teacher.

The first intent applies more readily to a formal classroom observation that includes a pre-observation conference in which the teacher and principal agree on a focus for the classroom observation. The predetermined focus drives the classroom observation and the techniques used to collect data.

During an informal classroom observation, the principal develops a focus on the spot, and this is why the principal is more than a mere observer. The principal becomes a silent but active participant, making a snap judgment about what to focus on and for how long. The broad focus of the classroom observation is dependent on what occurs in the classroom. Figure 3.1 examines some possibilities that the principal might focus on during an informal classroom observation.

Figure 3.1 Focus Areas for Informal Classroom Observations

Broad Focus Area	*Possible Target Points Within the Focus Area*
Instructional methods and techniques	Cooperative learning, direct instruction, indirect instruction, questioning strategies, wait time
Organizing for instruction	Use of advance organizers, posing a problem, dilemma, or objective
Classroom procedures	Beginning and ending classroom procedures, transitions, physical proximity and movement
Student engagement and involvement	On- and off-task behavior, questioning strategies, use of student responses to extend discussion, maintaining student focus and attention
Subject matter and content	Organization, breadth, depth, scope
Other	Use of technology and manipulatives
Any combination of the above	

Teaching is not an isolated enterprise; one area of instruction (e.g., organizing for instruction) affects other areas (e.g., student engagement and involvement, classroom procedures). This is why the learning environment is exciting. Because teachers are engaged in the moments of teaching and make split-second decisions about what to do next based on student responses, they benefit from data, subsequent feedback, and opportunities to talk and reflect about teaching.

Types of Data

Data may be quantitative, qualitative, or a combination of both. Quantitative data include frequencies, distributions, and other counts or tallies of information. Checklists are quantitative because they do not use words to describe what occurred, how, or why. For example, the observer could use a checklist to tally how many questions were asked of children in the front row or how many times the teacher called on students whose hands were raised or not raised. Qualitative data could include scripted notes detailing patterns of activities, words, and other events observed. Whether data are quantitative or qualitative, accuracy is essential; the credibility of the process and the principal is at stake.

Types of Data and Data-Collection Techniques

On entering the classroom, the principal makes two major decisions:

1. Where to focus his or her attention during the observation
2. What observation technique(s) to use to display data that shed light on classroom practices

These two considerations are interrelated because what the observer decides to focus on during the observation dictates which technique or tool is most suitable for collecting data. Regardless of the technique for data collection, always start small by focusing on one or two items to be observed, and take notes that relate directly to the items. Remember: Less is more!

Figure 3.2 provides an overview of the techniques used to collect data while observing teachers.

Figure 3.2 Classroom Observation Data-Collection Techniques

Techniques	Description
Behavior category	A narrow set of behaviors is tracked.
Checklist	A standardized form allows the principal to check which activities and behaviors are present or absent.
Classroom diagramming	Classroom tracking of certain behaviors or movement of teachers and students are recorded in short increments of time.
Selected verbatim notes	Words, questions, and interactions are recorded verbatim.
Open narrative	Anecdotal notes with or without a focus are recorded.
Teacher-designed instrument	Teacher develops an instrument to audit certain teaching and learning behaviors.
Audiotape	The principal audiotapes the classroom, often taking notes or diagramming movement. The audio recording can be used to help reconstruct the events of the lesson.
Videotape	The events of the classroom are videotaped and then viewed at a later time.

Wide-Angle and Narrow-Angle Methods

Acheson and Gall (1997) developed a series of data-collection tools that are classified as either wide-angle methods or narrow-angle methods, similar to the lenses available for use on a camera. In general, the *wide-angle methods* allow the principal to capture a larger picture, and the *narrow-angle methods* allow the principal to "zoom in" and collect more finite data focused on a one or two aspects. Figure 3.3 describes the six most commonly used data-collection tools developed by Acheson and Gall (1997).

Figure 3.3 Data-Collection Tools: An Overview of Methods

Type of Method/Lens	Data-Collection Tool	Focus
Narrow lens	Selective verbatim	Records words that were said by the teacher, the students, or both
Narrow lens	Verbal flow	Details the frequency of who spoke—how often and when
Narrow lens	At-task	Provides detail, noting periodically over time of who appears to be at-task
Narrow lens	Class traffic	Tracks the teachers' (or students') physical movement
Narrow lens	Interaction analysis	Provides detail about the types of statements made by either the teacher or the students
Wide lens	Anecdotal/global scan	Notes what was occurring overall in the classroom. This can become more judgmental unless the supervisor records just the facts.
Adapted from Acheson & Gall (1997).		

Narrow-Angle Methods and Tools

Narrow-angle data-collection methods have several tools, including selective verbatim, verbal flow, at-task, class traffic, interaction analysis. These tools help the supervisor to collect data that detail which students are engaged by focusing on very specific types of data: words, frequency of words, student or teacher movement, etc. For example, if the principal enters a classroom in which the teacher engages students in a question-and-answer session, it is ideal to focus on what types of questions are asked. The principal narrows the observation technique to chronicle in detail the questions asked of students. Therefore, the principal needs to write, as verbatim as possible, the questions asked. The scope of data collected would typically be just the questions; however, the lens can widen to track not only the questions the teacher asks, but also the students' responses to the questions (see Figure 4.1, Bloom's Taxonomy).

Wide-Angle Methods and Tools

The most prevalent wide-angle tool is the *global scan,* which is useful for collecting information about the events of the class as these events unfold. Data could include the words of the teacher and students, the physical activity of the teacher and students, the types of instructional methods used and their duration—or just about any other event or occurrence in the classroom. The global scan is intended to give the teacher a general sense of the classroom.

The strength of the wide-angle method of recording anecdotally is the ability to chronicle events as they occur. A weakness is the possibility that bias and value judgment may emerge as the events are being scripted. Consider the following two statements:

1. "While you were giving instructions for the small-group activity, one girl left her seat to sharpen a pencil."
2. "One girl sauntered to the pencil sharpener. From the smile on her face, she was mocking your rapid-fire approach to giving instructions."

The first statement presents the facts without editorial speculation. The second statement is value laden; even its wording ("sauntered" and "rapid-fire approach") sends a negative message. How is the teacher likely to respond to each statement? Using the wide-angle method of scripting anecdotally requires a conscious effort to leave value judgments off the page.

And Data Are Important Because...

Data collected during classroom observations tend to describe teacher and student behaviors using a series of snapshots, with each piece of data depicting isolated events that occurred during a teaching episode. It is the analysis of the data that permits the teacher and the supervisor to identify patterns through which a holistic image of teaching can be created. The key for success is to observe not only the teacher but also the students. Effective observation involves keeping one eye on the teacher and the other eye on the students, tracking the effect of teaching behaviors on student response and learning.

Show Me the Data!

Each data-collection tool has its strengths and limitations and yields different types of information about the events of the classroom observation. The following illustrates what data would look like using *select* data-collection tools described in Figure 3.3.

Selective verbatim focuses on specific words, questions, or responses of the teacher, students, or both. The first example focuses on the questions the teacher asks.

T: What were the events leading up to the crime?

T: Of these events, which event motivated the main character the most?

T: Why was this event the most important?

T: How would the ending of the book have been different if this event had not occurred?

The next example displays both the teacher's questions and the student's responses to the questions.

Teacher Questions		Student Responses	
1.	What were the events leading up to the crime?	1.	The man was desperate, he had to feed his children; he lost his job; his oldest son was diagnosed with a life-threatening disease.
2.	Of these events, which event motivated the main character the most?	2.	The son's life-threatening disease
3.	Why was this event the most important?	3.	He had no money to pay the doctor.

Another way the selective verbatim technique can be used is to categorize the teacher's responses as "praise," "correction," or "preventive prompt," followed by the time, as in the following example.[1] The data in the following example shed light not only on the teacher's statements but also on the patterns and routines for the beginning of the class period.

---

1 Developed by Theresa L. Benfante, Behavior Interventionist at Central Alternative School, Cobb County School District (Georgia). Used with permission.

Tool 3 Selective Verbatim

Teacher: *Bob Bennet*   Date of observation: *February 25, 2005*

Class: *Study and Life Skills*   Period of the day: *Morning*

Observer: *Pat Montalvo*

Time of observation: Start: *9:40*   End: *9:50*

Total time spent in observation: *10 minutes*

Number of students present: *11*   Grade level: *Sophomores*

Topic of the lesson: *Teacher was readying the class to begin work*

Teacher Comment/Response	Time	Praise	Correction	Preventive Prompt
Please come in and get seated.	9:40			X
Bob, close the door and come in.	9:41		X	
Your pencils need to be sharpened before class.	9:42		X	
Looks like Jeff is ready to get started.	9:43	X		
Jack needs to stop talking and follow along.	9:45		X	
Louise is patiently waiting for us to begin.	9:46	X		
Guys, you need to get paper out and follow along.	9:47		X	
I see Martin is ready!	9:48	X		
I can't begin until every ones' attention is up here.	9:49		X	
Tony, take your hood off your head please.	9:49		X	

Teacher Comment/Response	Time	Praise	Correction	Preventive Prompt
We have wasted 10 minutes waiting for some of you to get ready.	9:50		X	
Leslie is ready to go.		X		
Bob and Jack, we are waiting for you to pay attention.			X	
Thanks Steve, I see you are ready.		X		
When you come to class prepared, we can begin on time.			X	X
Ratio of praise to correction: 5:9				
Preventive prompts: 2				

Global scan/anecdotal focuses on events, actions, or words of the teacher, students, or both. Data that are scripted can take many forms. To chronicle the events, only a blank sheet of paper, an eye, and ear are needed to capture the events of the class. Anecdotal notes can focus events as they unfold by time or just by events.

Anecdotal Data Sample—by Time

9:05	Teacher asked student (male, red shirt) to elaborate on the "yes" response.... How S. E. Hinton developed the symbol of the Siamese fighting fish.
9:06	Student: "at the end of the story... he sets the rumble fish free and then he dies...the characters fight like the rumble fish."
9:07	Teacher asks a general question: "Are there are other examples throughout the book?" (several hands go up...teacher calls on student who is fidgeting with her backpack)

Anecdotal Data Sample—Series of Events, No Time

✓ Teacher was at the door when students entered the room.

✓ Students knew the routine: they went to their seats, pulled out books, notebooks, and the homework assignment due (the agenda on the blackboard cued students on what to do to get ready for the period).

✓ When the bell rang, a student turned on the overhead projector; teacher pointed to the math problem—students began working on solving the word problem.

✓ Teacher took attendance, spoke briefly with a student at her desk, and walked up and down the aisles collecting homework assignments.

✓ Teacher focused students on the word problem—asked for the properties of the word problem before asking for the solution.

✓ Student in the back of the room (arm in cast) gave the answer to the word problem—320 pounds of coffee beans.

✓ Teacher asked student in front of the room to write the formula she used to get a different answer (285 was her response).

✓ As the student wrote the formula, teacher asked questions of another student who had the same answer.

✓ Student at the board "talked through" her answer and the steps she took to derive the answer.

✓ The teacher enlisted other students for answers to questions.

✓ Teacher transitioned the class to a page in their books—modeled how to analyze the word problem—wrote numbers on the board, enlisted students with helping her with the computations.

Checklists

A more narrow data-collection method is the *checklist* approach, in which data are usually tallied at the end so that patterns can be inferred; however, checklist data also can be descriptive. A sample of checklist data is detailed in Tool 4.

Tool 4 Sample Checklist Classroom Observation Form

Teacher: *Nancy Chandley* Date of observation: *February 12, 2005*

Observer: *Martine Orozco*

Class: *English 1* Period of the day: *Block 2*

Time of observation: Start: *10:25* End: *10:45*

Total time spent in observation: *20 minutes*

Number of students present: *26* Grade level: *Freshman*

Topic of the lesson: *Writing narrative essays*

Students were

- ☐ working in small, cooperative groups
- ☐ making a presentation
- ☐ taking a test
- ☑ working independently at their desks
- ☐ viewing a film
- ☐ other _____

Teacher was

- ☐ lecturing
- ☐ facilitating a question and answer sequence
- ☑ working independently with students
- ☐ demonstrating a concept
- ☐ introducing a new concept
- ☐ reviewing for a test
- ☐ coming to closure
- ☐ other

Comments: Nancy:

- *Students were working independently at their desks.*
- *The rearrangement of the room (desk, podium, table) allowed you to work independently with students on their essays and to keep an eye on students working at their desks.*

Perhaps you should hold the next freshman-level meeting in your room so others can see your room arrangement.

Thanks for letting me visit your room and see the work you do to help our students become better writers. I appreciate your efforts.
—Martine Orozco

The strength of the checklist method is its ease of use; the principal takes in information and checks off what was observed or heard during the observation period. A weakness is that it is often difficult to reduce words or actions to a predetermined category on a checklist form. Moreover, checklist data—although easy to tally or look for patterns of occurrence of events (e.g., how many times students raised their hands, the number of questions asked)—can limit room for describing or giving specific detail about the events observed. The checklist has its place and enables the principal to be more efficient when making observations.

Mixed-Method Data-Collection Techniques

Combining scripted (anecdotal) and checklist methods provides both qualitative and quantitative data about what was observed. Tool 5 offers a sample of how both open-ended (scripted) and narrow (checklist) data can be combined to chronicle the events of the classroom.

Tool 5 Anecdotal and Checklist Data-Collection Method, Focus on Cooperative Learning

Teacher: *Ms. Janie Adams*   Date of observation: *April 25, 2005*

Observer: *Dr. Antonio Tanuta*

Class: *U. S. History*   Period of the day: *2nd period*

Time of observation: Start: *9:05*   End: *9:25*

Total time spent in observation: *20 minutes*

Number of students present: *26*   Grade level: *Juniors*

Topic of the lesson: *Examining how a bill is passed*

Focus on Cooperative Learning	Presence or Absence	Notes
Objectives for the cooperative learning group	*X*	■ *Objective for the activity was written on the whiteboard.* ■ *Teacher referred to the objective as students asked questions.* ■ *Teacher returned to the objective during closure of group activity.*
Clarity of directions	*X*	■ *Before breaking students into groups, teacher gave directions.* ■ *Teacher distributed directions for each group once students moved into their groups.*
Movement into groups	*X*	■ *Six minutes for students to move into groups* ■ *Materials were bundled for each group in advance of movement*
Monitoring and intervening strategies	*X*	■ *Teacher turned lights on and off to get attention.* ■ *Teacher broke into group time three times with clarifying directions.* ■ *Teacher visited each group four times.*

Focus on Cooperative Learning	Presence or Absence	Notes
Evaluation strategies		
Interaction with students	x	■ *Asked questions and gave feedback to groups while monitoring* ■ *Clarified directions* ■ *Became a member of each group*
Follow-up instruction— large-group processing	x	■ *After 23 minutes, teacher called end to group work.* ■ *Students moved desks and chairs back in order.* ■ *Group reporter gave report.* ■ *Teacher asked and answered questions.*

Tool 6 presents an open-ended form for collecting data in a foreign language classroom.[2]

2 Developed by Marcia Wilbur, Ph.D., Head of World Languages and Cultures Professional Development at the College Board, based on her work at Gull Lake High School Foreign Language Department, Richland, Michigan. Used with permission.

Tool 6 Foreign Language Observation Checklist

Teacher: *Mary Smith*   Date of observation: *4/12/05*

Observer: *Fred Jones*

Class: *French 2*   Period of the day: *4*

Time of observation: Start *12:30*   End: *12:50*

Total time spent in observation: *20 minutes*

Number of students present: *28*   Grade level: *9 & 10*

Topic of the lesson: *French teenagers*

1. Are all language modalities evident in the lesson (speaking, writing, listening, and reading) as well as culture?

   - *Students heard a passage read by the teacher, then spoke with a partner or in a group of three to collectively summarize (in writing) the gist of the reading.*

   - *Because the passage was about French teens, culture was evident.*

2. Does the teacher use a wide variety of prepared and authentic materials at appropriate levels?

   - *The reading was taken from an authentic French source—a Parisian teen magazine.*

   - *Students were able to recreate the gist, so the level was apparently suitable for these learners.*

3. Is the purpose of each activity clearly explained to the students?

   - *The activity had already just begun when I entered. However, students seemed to have a clear understanding of what they were doing.*

4. Does the teacher model activities when giving directions and check for comprehension afterward?

   - *Mary gave directions before and after each of the two times she read the passage.*

   - *When students had finished rewriting the passage summaries, three groups shared their summaries aloud with the class, and class members commented on the* accuracy of information, making suggestions to augment, improve, and/or clarify the content of each.

- *Mary validated the information given, praised the students for their good work, and made suggestions for improvement.*

5. Are the transitions between activities smooth?
   - *I only observed the passage summary activity.*
   - *The class was preparing to move to a new activity when I left the room.*
   - *The steps in the summary activity went smoothly from one to the next.*

6. Are the students on task and actively involved in the learning process?
   - *Most students worked cooperatively with their partners.*
   - *I noticed that there were three groups of three. In two of those groups, one student appeared to be much less involved than the other two students in the grouping.*
   - *Because only one student was writing per group, I suggest breaking up the groups of three and sticking to pairs for this particular activity so that as many students as possible are highly engaged in the process.*

7. Is there an appropriate use of partner–pair or small group activities?
   - *Yes, students worked in pairs (or groups of three as described above) with some brief moments of teacher-centered talk for the reading, directions, and feedback.*

The Seating Chart

An efficient way to collect data is to use the seating chart. Generic seating charts can be made in advance, or teachers can be asked to provide a general seating chart of their rooms at the beginning of the year. Several techniques for observing student and teacher behaviors make good use of the seating chart to collect data. Advantages for using the seating chart to chronicle data include the following:

- Ease of use: A seating chart can be drawn within half a minute of entering the room.

- ◆ Amount of data: A large amount of information can be recorded on a single chart. (Consider breaking up the observation into five minute increments—it is easy to get five minutes' worth of data on a single seating chart).
- ◆ Focus on the events: Important aspects of student behavior can be recorded while observing the teacher and the class as a whole.

If using the seating chart, it makes sense to have 15 to 20 copies available. The following generic seating chart (Tool 7) will assist you in collecting data.

Tool 7 Seating Chart

Teacher: _____ Date of observation: _____

Class: _____ Period of the day: _____

Observer: _____

Time of observation: Start: _____End: _____

Total time spent in observation: _____

Number of students present: _____ Grade level: _____

Topic of the lesson: _____

File Cabinet

Teacher's Desk

Some examples of data that can be recorded easily on a seating chart include

◆ student–teacher question patterns

◆ reinforcement and feedback

◆ classroom movement patterns

Using the seating chart to track question patterns can provide data on whether the teacher focuses only on a few students on one side of the room. The seating chart also can be used to track classroom movement patterns to determine whether the teacher lectures from the front of the room only, or the types and frequency of feedback and reinforcement given to students.

Use Technology to Assist with Tracking Classroom Observation Data

Technology provides opportunities for principals to use a Palm Pilot to track information. Software is now available to let the principal enter data on a handheld device, import the data to a laptop, and then print out data collected during a classroom observation. Written follow-up notes before a post-observation conference can be provided using e-mail.

Looking Ahead...

The next chapter explores data-collection tools that the principal can use while stepping out to observe teachers.

4

Looking in
While Stepping Out

In This Chapter...

◆ Data collection tools and their applications

Teachers want the facts; they need to be able to examine and reflect on what these data mean during follow-up conversations with the principal (see Chapter 5). Understanding and applying the tools of data collection, the principal has firm footing to conduct informal observations that can help teachers focus on their classroom practices.

Data-Collection Tools and Their Application

Several tools are available and detailed here that will help principals track data from informal classroom observations. Unless indicated, the tools in this section are modified from *The Principal as Instructional Leader* (Zepeda, 2003). To illustrate these applications, each description includes the following:

◆ background

◆ observation focus

◆ observation technique

◆ explanation of the tool and technique

◆ how and why the technique is helpful

- directions and approaches for using the tool
- where appropriate, alternative data-collection strategies
- tips for using the technique

The following data-collection tools can help you track data from classroom observations. Principals are encouraged to use their imagination and revise these forms to develop unique renditions based on the context of the classroom—subject areas, grade levels, and the personnel teaching (e.g., teacher and paraprofessional, regular and special education coteaching partners). As a reminder, there are two decisions that are made when entering a classroom during an informal classroom observation:

1. Where to focus the observation based on what is occurring in the classroom
2. What data-collection tool or strategy to use to capture a rich portrayal of the events of the classroom

Given that this book is promoting informal classroom observations, the principal who is out and about will be more likely to conduct several informal classroom observations a day; therefore, tracking critical information about each observation is important. For each informal classroom observation, the following information should be noted in addition to the data collected during the observation:

- teacher name
- date of the observation
- observer
- class
- period of the day
- total time spent in observation
- beginning time of the observation
- ending time of the observation
- number of students present
- grade level
- topic of the lesson

This information is helpful when following up with the teacher and tracking which teachers are being observed and when. As a time-management strategy, this information helps the principal to determine the time of the day observations are occurring. For example, at the end of a month, the principal is able to determine whether more informal classroom observations were conducted in the morning or the afternoon or whether the observations were evenly distributed throughout the day. Moreover, such a tracking system ensures that all teachers benefit from informal classroom observations.

Observation Guide Using Bloom's Taxonomy

Background

Teachers spend much time talking with students—lecturing, giving directions, and asking and answering questions. To ensure understanding and application of knowledge, teachers commonly engage students in question-and-answer sessions (also referred to as Q&A). Questions can prompt responses ranging from simple recall of information to abstract processes of applying, synthesizing, and evaluating information. Bloom (1956) and his colleagues developed a continuum for categorizing questions and responses. Bloom's taxonomy includes the following elements, arranged from lowest to highest order:

- ◆ Knowledge: recalling specific facts
- ◆ Comprehension: describing in one's own words
- ◆ Application: applying information to produce some result
- ◆ Analysis: subdividing something to show how it is put together
- ◆ Synthesis: creating a unique, original product
- ◆ Evaluation: making value decisions about issues

Bloom's Taxonomy frames the analysis of both written and oral questions. Figure 4.1 provides an overview of Bloom's taxonomy of questioning. Note that the continuum represents lower-order to higher-order thinking.

Figure 4.1 Bloom's Taxonomy

Bloom's Taxonomy and Definition	Sample Verb Stems	Students' Responses Would Indicate Skills Such As
Lowest Order		
Knowledge/Recall: Students are asked to remember information.	Summarize, describe, interpret	Memorizing, recognizing, identifying, and recalling.
Comprehension: Students demonstrates they have understanding to organize and arrange material.	Classify, discuss, explain, identify, indicate, locate, report, restate, review, translate	Interpreting; translating from one medium to another; describing in one's own words; organizing and selecting facts and ideas.
Application: Students apply previously learned information to reach an answer to a different but similar problem.	Apply, choose, demonstrate, dramatize, employ, illustrate, interpret, operate, practice, schedule, sketch, solve	Solving problems; applying information to produce an end product.
Application: Students apply previously learned information to reach an answer to a different but similar problem.	Apply, choose, demonstrate, dramatize, employ, illustrate, interpret, operate, practice, schedule, sketch, solve	Solving problems; applying information to produce an end product.
Analysis: Students critically examine events and perform certain operations such as separating whole to part or part to whole.	Analyze, calculate, categorize, compare, contrast, criticize, differentiate, discriminate, examine, question	Subdividing, find'ng, identifying, and separating a whole into parts.

Bloom's Taxonomy and Definition	Sample Verb Stems	Students' Responses Would Indicate Skills Such As
Synthesis: Students produce an original work, make predictions, and/or solve problems.	Arrange, create, assemble, design, compose, develop, construct, formulate, manage, organize, plan, prepare, propose	Creating an original production.
Highest Order		
Evaluation: Students answer a question that does not have an absolute answer, provide an educated guess about the solution to a problem, or render a judgment or opinion with backup support.	Appraise, argue, assess, attach, defend, judge, rate, support, value, evaluate.	Making a decision, prioritizing information, drawing a conclusion.

Observation focus: Questioning strategies based on the class discussion

Observation technique: Selective verbatim

Explanation of the tool and technique: Selective verbatim is a narrow-lens tool that allows the observer to focus on select words of the teacher, the student, or both.

How and why the technique is helpful: This technique is helpful to give teacher's feedback about the types of questions and the frequency of the types of questions asked. This technique can also assist the teacher in examining the levels of understanding and comprehension of content based on student responses. This technique can also shed light on the proportion of higher and lower order questions asked over a specified time.

Directions and approaches for using the tool: Using Tool 8, the principal records only the questions the teacher asks of students. Write the sentence in the left-hand column. Put a check in the box that best describes the cognitive level of the question. (This may be part of the post-observation conference.)

Tips:

- During the observation, write the question, and then in the post-observation conference, have the teacher identify the level of thinking for each question noted.

- An alternative strategy is to ask the teacher to rework a lower-order question into a higher-level question. Go back and forth.

- Another way to landscape data using a more wide-angle lens related to teacher questions and the level of questions is presented in Tool 9.

Tool 8 Observation Guide Using Bloom's Taxonomy

Teacher: *Ms. Anita Rodriguez*   Date of observation: *April 2, 2005*

Observer: *Frank Lewis*

Class: *4th grade*   Period of the day: *Morning Block*

Time of observation: Start: *10:10*   End: *10:30*

Total time spent in observation: *20 minutes*

Number of students present: *17*   Grade level: *4th grade*

Topic of the lesson: *Decimals*

Time	Questions and Activities	Levels of Thinking					
		KNOWLEDGE	COMPREHENSION	APPLICATION	ANALYSIS	SYNTHESIS	EVALUATION
10:10	*How many have heard the word decimal?*	✓					
	What do you think decimals mean?	✓					
	How do you know?	✓					
	Have you ever seen a decimal?	✓					
	What do you think that means?	✓					
	Why the decimal? Why that period?	✓					

Time	Questions and Activities	Levels of Thinking					
		K N O W L E D G E	C O M P R E H E N S I O N	A P P L I C A T I O N	A N A L Y S I S	S Y N T H E S I S	E V A L U A T I O N
10:15	Decimal points do what?	✓					
	What makes the cents, not the dollar?	✓					
	Why is 99 cents not a dollar?		✓				
10:25	How would you write $200?	✓					
	What does "00" mean?	✓					
	Is that where Desmond saw a decimal point?	✓					
	What instrument...temperature?	✓					
	How many kinds of therm? Name 2.	✓					
10:30	What is she looking for?	✓					
	What is a normal temperature?	✓					
	Have you seen your temperature written?	✓					
	Why do you think you need to use a decimal point?		✓				

Tool 9 Alternative Observation Guide Using Bloom's Taxonomy

Teacher: *Ms. Anita Rodriguez*   Date of observation: *April 2, 2005*

Observer: *Frank Lewis*

Class: *4th grade*   Period of the day: *Morning Block*

Time of observation: Start: *10:10*   End: *10:30*

Total time spent in observation: *20 minutes*

Number of students present: *17*   Grade level: *4th grade*

Topic of the lesson: *Decimals*

Time	Teacher Questions	Taxonomy Level
8:10	How many have heard the word "decimal"?	
	What do you think decimals mean?	
	How do you know?	
	Have you ever seen a decimal?	
	What do you think that means?	
	Why the decimal? Why that period?	
10:15	Decimal points do what?	
	What makes the cents, not the dollar?	
	Why is 99 cents not a dollar?	
10:25	How would you write $200?	
	What does "00" mean?	
	Is that where Desmond saw a decimal point?	
	What instrument...temperature?	
	How many kinds of therm? Name 2.	
10:30	What is she looking for?	
	What is a normal temperature?	
	Have you seen your temperature written?	
	Why do you think you need to use a decimal point?	

Focusing on Wait Time

Background

A staple in teaching is the lecture and discussion, in which student response carries the rate and pace of the experience. Teachers, noticing cues from students, make adjustments in the pace and pitch of the classroom discussion. At the heart of lecture, discussion, and group processing of knowledge is the asking of questions. How the teacher responds to questions is important for two reasons: The quality of response is related to wait time, and the quality of the answer is related to wait time. Stahl (1994, pp. 3–5) related that when students are given three seconds or more of undisturbed wait time, there are certain positive outcomes:

- The length and correctness of their responses increase.
- The number of their "I don't know" and no answer responses decreases.
- The number of volunteered, appropriate answers by larger numbers of students greatly increases.
- Students' scores on academic achievement tests tend to increase.
- When teachers wait patiently in silence for three seconds or more at appropriate places, positive changes in their own teacher behaviors also occur.
- Teachers' questioning strategies tend to be more varied and flexible.
- Teachers decrease the quantity and increase the quality and variety of their questions.
- Teachers ask additional questions that require more complex information processing and higher-level thinking on the part of students.

From the research of Stahl and others (e.g., Rowe, 1986), wait time is think time, and 3 seconds has been reported as the ideal amount of time to wait for student response.

Observation focus: Wait time during class discussion or lecture

Observation technique: Wide-angle approach that focuses on not so much the questions but the wait time between the time the teacher finishes the question and a student is called on the answer the question

Explanation of the tool and technique: Once the teacher completes articulating the question, track the wait time afforded before calling on a student to answer the question.

How and why the technique is helpful: This tool can help the teacher to focus on the amount of wait time between the question and the response while examining the complexity of questions. This type of data can help the teacher and observer examine student engagement, understanding of concepts, and the pace of questions asked.

Directions and approaches for using the tool: Using a watch with a second hand, note the time the teacher waits from completing the question to calling on a student. Note as much of the question as possible, focusing more on the end words of the question.

Tip:

- ◆ Have the teacher examine the types of questions and examine the amount of wait time afforded to students to answer the questions.

Tool 10 Focus on Wait Time

Teacher: *Mr. Haidong Chen*   Date of observation: *April 18, 2005*

Observer: *Francesca Duncan*

Class: *English 7*   Period of the day: *Period 1*

Time of observation: Start: *8:05*   End: *8:20*

Total time spent in observation: *15 minutes*

Number of students present: *24*   Grade level: *Grade 9*

Topic of the lesson: *S. E. Hinton's Rumble Fish*

Teacher Question	Wait Time (seconds)
... in what year? ... James?	2 seconds
When you think of the lessons the characters learned by the end of the book, who do you think grew up the most?	3 seconds
How does the Siamese fighting fish come to be symbolic of the characters in this book?	5 seconds
Leslie, are there any other symbols?	4 seconds
Do these other symbols relate to the importance of the Siamese fighting fish?	2 seconds
Why do you support S. E. Hinton chose Siamese fighting fish rather than another type of domestic fish?	6 seconds

Another way to track wait time is to landscape data by including the taxonomy level of the questions related to wait time. This type of data can enhance analysis and reflection by examining both the type of questions using Bloom's Taxonomy and the amount of wait time.

Tool 11 Wait Time with Bloom's Taxonomy for Examining Levels of Questions

Teacher: *Mr. Haidong Chen*   Date of observation: *April 18, 2005*

Observer: *Francesca Duncan*

Class: *English 7*   Period of the day: *Period 1*

Time of observation: Start: *8:05*   End: *8:20*

Total time spent in observation: *15 minutes*

Number of students present: *24*   Grade level: *Grade 9*

Topic of the lesson: *S. E. Hinton's Rumble Fish*

Teacher Question	Wait Time (seconds)	Question Domain
...in what year?... James?	*2 seconds*	*Knowledge*
When you think of the lessons the characters learned by the end of the book, who do you think grew up the most?	*3 seconds*	*Synthesis, Evaluation*
How does the Siamese fighting fish come to be symbolic of the characters in this book?	*5 seconds*	*Evaluation*
Is there any deeper meaning to letting the fish out of their tanks at the end of the story?	*3 seconds*	*Evaluation*

Tips:

- ◆ Suggest the teacher analyze wait time in terms of the type of question asked.
- ◆ Leave the "Question Domain" column blank and let the teacher fill in the level of taxonomy.
- ◆ If there is an overreliance on lower-level domains, role play with the teacher to rephrase the questions to move toward higher-order domains.

Cause and Effect

Observation focus: Tracking teacher behaviors to determine the effects they have on students

Observation technique: Wide-angle lens technique that examines teachers' actions and words and the effects they have on students

Explanation of the tool and technique: This tool is designed to give the principal and the teacher information concerning the influence of the teacher's actions on students' responses in the classroom. This tool can be useful in observing a teacher's classroom management, direction giving, and other teacher behaviors related to student response.

How and why the technique is helpful: This type of information can be especially helpful for new teachers or teachers who are experiencing difficulties with classroom management (student behavior, managing learning activities, and transitions). This tool gives the teacher information about the influence of the teacher's actions on student responses. This tool can be useful in observing a teacher's classroom management, questioning strategies, direction giving, and other teacher behaviors that ask for a student response.

Directions and approaches for using the tool: Divide a blank sheet of paper into two columns. Record teacher actions in the left-hand column and record student responses to these actions in the right-hand column.

Tip:
- Focus on concrete actions, directions, or words of the teacher and the effect they have on student response or behavior.

Tool 12 Cause and Effect

Teacher: *Mr. James Ackman* Date of observation: *May 5, 2005*
Observer: *Dr. Juanita Powell*
Class: *Accounting 1*   Period of the day: *6th period*
Time of observation: Start: *1:15*   End: *1:35*
Total time spent in observation: *20 minutes*
Number of students present: *26* Grade level: *Mixed (Juniors and Seniors)*
Topic of the lesson: *Using Accounting Software*

Teacher	Student Response or Activity
Bell (1:15)	Milling around room
Takes roll Makes announcements Collects homework	Quietly talking
Turns on overhead and says, "Take out your notebooks and open your book to page 140."	Students pull out materials. Red shirt slapping boy next to him (Blue shirt)
"Folks, heads up to the overhead and focus on the chapter objectives." Begins stating the objectives for the chapter.	Shuffling to get their books out and open to page 140. Seven students (out of 16) do not have books.
"Read from pages 140 to 145." Teacher sitting at desk getting software to boot up for a demonstration	Students without books: Two are talking with each other Two are sleeping Three are reading from nearby student's books
"Who would like to offer a summary while I get the program loaded?"	Four students are still reading; three students (who did not have book) are talking with their neighbors; two students sleeping; four students raise their hands; one student asks a question out loud, "How can you expect us to finish reading five pages in 10 minutes," and another student blurts, "bite me."
"James, repeat what you said."	James: "bite me."
"James, I just cannot believe you said, 'bite me.' Are you talking to me?"	Yeah, yeah, just "get bit," Roberts.
Pushes the call button for assistance.	Eight students talking; three laughing, James walks to the door

Variety of Instructional Methods

Background

Regardless of subject area, grade level, or the teacher's experience, a single class period should include a variety of instructional methods. Research has cast new light on the way children learn, and can we no longer assume that any one instructional strategy is sufficient to reach *all* learners *all* of the time. Effective teachers not only use a variety of instructional strategies but also differentiate strategies. To differentiate, teachers provide alternative approaches to the methods used to present content and the ways that students show mastery of learning objectives. Given the myriad ability levels of students and the recognition that no two learners learn at the same rate or way, differentiated instruction shows great promise as a way of thinking about teaching and learning. In a classroom in which instruction is differentiated, students are offered a variety of ways to learn. According to Tomlinson (1999, p. 2), differentiated instruction flourishes when the following occur:

- teachers begin where the students are
- teachers engage students in instruction through different learning modalities
- Students compete more against themselves than against others
- teachers provide specific ways for each individual to learn
- teachers use classroom time flexibly
- teachers are diagnosticians, prescribing the best possible instruction for each student

Observation focus: Variety of instructional techniques

Observation technique: Narrow-angle lens technique focusing on the number of instructional strategies, the length of each, and the activities students engage in during each

Explanation of the tool and technique: For each instructional strategy used, indicate the time and what the teacher and the students are doing. Additional information such as transitions also could be noted. Tracking variety of instructional strategies will require a loner classroom observation, perhaps an entire class period; however, it is not outside of the realm of possibility for the principal to observe in a classroom where more than one instructional technique is used in a 15–20 minute span of time.

How and why the technique is helpful: This technique can give insight about the number and duration of instructional strategies used during a class segment.

Tips:

- Note teacher cues for each strategy and the transitions from one method or activities used to further the method.
- Note the length of each strategy.

Tool 13 Variety of Instructional Materials

Teacher: *Ms. Shelly Better*   Date of observation: *March 4, 2005*

Observer: *Jaime Escobar*

Class: *English 1 (Remedial)*   Period of the day: *Block 1*

Time of observation: Start: *9:00*   End: *10:10*

Total time spent in observation: *70 minutes*

Number of students present: *25*   Grade level: *9th grade*

Topic of the lesson: *S. E. Hinton's <u>Rumble Fish</u>*

Time	Instructional Method	Teacher Behavior	Student Activities
9:00–9:10	Organizing lecture	Lecture, directions for small group work, break students into small groups	Listening, taking notes, asking questions
9:11–9:35	Cooperative learning	Assist students to get into small groups, passing out materials; monitoring student work	Getting into groups, selecting roles (recorder, timer)
9:36–9:48	Large-group discussion	Leading students to citations offered by groups	Discussing the symbol, the Siamese fighting fish; finding citations from the text to support ideas; group recorder presenting citations from the text in support of ideas; reading citations offered by other groups
9:49–9:59	Question and answer	Ask questions	Responding to questions (looking up citations to back up ideas); asking questions, begin homework assignment
10:00–10:10	Closure	Assignment given	

Examining Teacher–Student Discussion with a Focus on How Student Comments Are Incorporated into the Lesson

Background

Nothing keeps a class moving forward more than a lively discussion in which student responses are incorporated into the lesson. Teachers who incorporate student responses into lessons extend learning and are able to check more readily for understanding. Student responses also serve to assess student learning, giving cues to the connections students are making with content, their ability to apply what they are learning, and the areas that need to be reinforced or retaught. When a teacher incorporates student comments, such behavior signals a student-centered classroom in which student questions often serve to extend the concepts that are being studied.

Observation focus: Incorporating student comments and ideas into the discussion

Observation technique: Narrow focus using selective verbatim

Explanation of the tool and technique: This tool is designed to give the principal and the teacher information concerning how teachers incorporate student comments into class discussions.

How and why the technique is helpful: This technique can also be helpful in helping teachers to assess student learning based on student response and to become aware of the information student response can give relative to understanding and application of concepts previously taught.

Directions and approaches for using the tool: Note what the teacher says (focusing on questions), the student response to the question, and then what the teacher does with the student response.

Tip:
- Given the fast nature of classroom discussions, writing question stems (e.g., "Can we find examples from the text…") will suffice.

Tool 14 Examining Teacher–Student Discussion
with a Focus on How Student Comments
Are Incorporated into the Lesson

Teacher: *Mr. Jack Howard*   Date of observation: *April 27, 2005*

Observer: Jeannette Geter

Class: *English 7*   Period of the day: *2nd period*

Time of observation: Start: *8:50*   End: *9:06*

Total time spent in observation: *16 minutes*

Number of students present: *25*   Grade level: *9th grade (Honors)*

Topic of the Lesson: *Symbolism found in S. E. Hinton's <u>Rumble Fish</u>*

Time	Teacher Talk/Question	Student Response	How Student Comments Are Used
8:50	A symbol is an object that represents something else. What are the symbols in <u>Rumble Fish</u>?	SR1: Siamese rumble fish	Can you expand on this? (Max asks)
		SR2: The gangs are made up of people who can't get along with one another.	Cite an example of this from the text?
8:53		SR3: See page 47.	Relate this to the end of the book.
8:55		SR4: At the end, the Siamese fighting fish are let go.	Does this parallel the death of the character?
8:57	In your opinion, was letting the fish go an act of bravery?	SR5: He was making a statement about being free...on page 98 it says he was born in the wrong era	OK, but was this act bravery or an act of cowardice?
9:01			What do you think the narrator meant by the "wrong era?"

Time	Teacher Talk/Question	Student Response	How Student Comments Are Used
		SR6: He just did not fit into the world he lives	What made him an outcast?
9:06	Can we find examples from the text that back up the idea he did not fit into the world he lives?		

Focus on Tracking Transition Patterns

Background

The transition is, in a sense, an instructional method. Smooth transitions conserve time, help to keep students focused on learning objectives, and lessen opportunities for classroom disruptions. Through advanced planning, transitions are enhanced when materials are ready to lessen the loss of time between activities or when moving from one method of instruction to another. Transitions are seamless, with students assuming some responsibility for efficient operation. Transitions are a more seamless instructional technique when teachers do the following:

- establish and reinforce routines aligned with the needs of learners
- cue students to a transition so they are ready to transition to the next activity
- have materials (handouts, materials, equipment) readily available before the transition begins
- provide clear directions as part of the transition

Observation focus: Transition strategies

Observation technique: Narrow angle focusing only on the transitions that a teacher uses between activities or instructional segments

Explanation of the tool and technique: The principal tracks which techniques the teacher uses between instructional segments—or in other words, how the teacher gets students from point A to point B.

How and why this technique is helpful: This technique helps the teacher to examine how activities and instruction are organized and the amount of time it takes to move from one activity to another. For teachers who might be having difficulty with student behavior, this strategy can assist teachers in improving their classroom-management technique.

Directions and approaches for using the tool: Record broadly the instructional activity and then the transition (cues, clarity of directions) used to move students from one activity to another, focusing on student responses based on the transition strategy.

Tool 15 Focus on Tracking Transition Patterns

Teacher: *Mrs. Cheryl Hofer*   Date of observation: *January 18, 2005*

Observer: *Dr. June Kaufman*

Class: *3rd grade (Math)*   Period of the day: *Morning*

Time of observation: Start: *10:10*   End: *10:24*

Total time spent in observation: *14 minutes*

Number of students present: *18*   Grade level: *4th grade*

Topic of the Lesson: *Map activity—geography*

Instruction/Activity	Transition	Student Response
10:10–10:14 Getting students into cooperative groups	*Gives directions for small cooperative group. Stops movement to give clarifying instructions. Hands out worksheets, maps, and other supplies.*	*Students meander, finding their group members; four students ask clarifying questions during movement.*
	Teacher directs team captains to pick up direction sheet for their groups.	
	Materials are packaged on teacher's desk; packets have a number on them corresponding to the group (e.g., 1, 2, 3).	
10:15–10:24 Students are working in groups. Teacher is walking from group to group redirecting students, answering questions.		
10:20 Teacher reminds students that they have four minutes left to complete task.		
10:24 Getting students back into large group	*Flicks lights on and off, asks Group 1 to send their rep to the front of the room to give a summary.*	*Students are moving desks, bringing*

Tracking Student Behavior

Background

Tracking student behavior helps teachers who are experiencing classroom-management issues, regardless of the teacher's experience level. However, observing student behavior is not necessarily related to discipline issues. Teachers establish classroom routines, plan lessons, organize materials, and interact with students with the best of intentions. Teachers can benefit from data about student behavior, and data can help teachers to pinpoint areas to be more aware of as they manage instruction, learning objectives, activities, and interactions with students. Data that clearly focus on student behavior and classroom- and instructional-management techniques can yield a fuller understanding of the complexities of teaching.

Observation focus: Student behavior

Observation technique: Narrow focus broadly applied to tracking student behavior during instruction—directions, verbal and nonverbal cues from the teacher and student response

Explanation of the tool and technique: This tool will help the observer to focus on teacher behaviors and their effect on student behavior and response.

How and why the technique is helpful: With the fast-paced nature of instruction, sometimes teachers cannot readily analyze the effect their words have on student behavior. This tool can assist the teacher in analyzing what is said and how students respond to what is being said, in addition to overall classroom management.

Directions and approaches for using the tool: Track teacher behavior (words, routines, activities, directions, etc.) and then immediately note student behavior.

Tip:

◆ Encourage the teacher to look for patterns of words and student behaviors.

Tool 16 Tracking Student Behavior

Teacher: Samuel Ortiz   Date of observation: May 6, 2005

Observer: Martin Scott

Class: 6th grade   Period of the day: Afternoon

Time of observation: Start: 2:20 End: 2:35

Total time spent in observation: 15 minutes

Number of students present: 18   Grade level: 6th grade

Topic of the lesson: Language arts (Verbs)

	Teacher	&	Student
1 2:20	Look at the Word of the Day on the board and write a sentence using the word. The word today is catastrophe.	1	Just one sentence or two?
2 2:20	One sentence, like we do every day.	2	We didn't do a word yesterday.
3 2:20	OK, then, like the one we did a few days ago.	3	
4 2:21	Tom, read your sentence.	4	I'm not done...I came in late.
5 2:22	Randy, let's hear your sentence.	5	My pen is out of ink...I can say the sentence I would have written.
6 2:22	Randy, this is the third time this week you have not come to class prepared to work.	6	Yeah, yeah, yeah. I only have pencils.
7 2:22	That's right...you can only use a pen to write class notes.	7	I don't like pens...you can't erase the marks.
8 2:23	Pens are what you must use...What don't you understand about this?	8	Why can't I use a pencil...Mrs. Scott lets us use pencils ... so does all my teachers, but you.

	Teacher	&	Student
9 2:23	That's right, young man, stand out in the hall for the next 15 minutes. Go to the office...now.	9	
10 2:24	Does anyone want to read their sentence?	10	Three hands go up
11 2:25	Leslie, go ahead and read your sentence.	11	After several attempts, the sailors were able to avoid a catastrophe at sea.
12 2:25	Excellent sentence, Leslie.	12	
13 2:26	Pull out your grammar books and go to page 89. Make sure your notebooks are ready for class notes.	13	Students begin to pull out books from book bags. Two students (girls in third row, far right) begin to pull at a book); students to their right exchange books and a notebook.
14 2:29	Go to Sentence 5, "The children seated at the table began asking for dessert." Look at the word "seated." Can this word be the verb in this sentence?	14	Hands go up, teacher asks Joey (his hand not raised) to answer the question. Laughter with other hands starting to go up.
15 2:29	Joey, what is your answer?	15	Yes.
16 2:29	Why all the laughter? And Joey, look at the sentence again.	16	
17 2:30	What is a participle?	17	About nine hands go up; four students looking in book for the answer; five students looking around the room.
18 2:31	Anna	18	A word that ends in ed, "en," "n," or "ing."
19 2:31		19	Boy shouts out "Not

	Teacher	&	Student
20 2:32	Tony, why "not"	20	What about "the man died"—isn't died a verb in that sentence and it ends in "ed"? Students in the third row are talking.
21 2:33	That's right in the sentence you gave Tony. But look back at Sentence 5…The word is "seated." The word "seated" is really functioning as what? Teacher does not call on students to answer…she begins to "teach" Let's consider a few points: ■ Pure grammatical rules do not always apply—you have to look at the sentence and how each word is being used. ■ A participle is more than a word that has a certain ending. A participle is usually a multi-worded adjective… ■ Let's look at the proof to determine if a word is an adjective.	21	Hands fly up…students want to answer…they are making sounds (ooh, ooh, ohh).
22 2:35	What is the proof to see if a word is an adjective?	22	Jackson answers: Whose, which, what kind of, how many.

Tracking the Beginning and Ending (Closure) of Class

Background

Effective teachers engage in bell-to-bell instruction. The first few minutes and the last few minutes are known to be two critically important points of time. Research shows that time wasted at the beginning and ending of class can never really be recouped; once time is lost, it is gone. Effective teachers establish daily routines for beginning and ending class. Grade level dictates the types of routines established. Although there are vast differences among elementary, middle, and high school classrooms, all share a commonality: the need for routines to begin and end instruction.

Beginning Class Routines

Teachers who have routines for the beginning of a class period use the time immediately before the tardy bell for getting students ready and organized for learning. Strategies to maximize time on task and to reduce "empty air time" before formal instruction begin include the following:

- taking attendance as students are entering the room
- having a "sponge" activity for students to start working on as they are getting ready for class to start. Sponge activities, purposefully short but related to the overall lesson and course content, "soak up" those extra few minutes at the beginning or ending of class that otherwise would be wasted. Sponge activities may include a math problem to be solved, a sentence to diagram, a vocabulary word to include in a sentence, or a short quiz.
- posting a daily agenda detailing the lesson objectives and what materials to get ready before the bell rings
- distributing class materials and collecting homework

All of these activities help to prepare students so that the moment the bell rings, instruction or other activities related to the lesson can begin.

Ending Class Routines

Effective teachers use the time immediately before the ending of a class period to recapitulate lessons learned and to help bring closure to the class activities. They relate what needs to be done to prepare for the next day so that once the bell rings, students can be dismissed. Different cues give students time to put away supplies and equipment and get ready to leave the class in an orderly manner.

Observation focus: Activities within the first 15 minutes of class beginning or the 15 minutes before the ending of the class.

Observation technique: Narrow focus using anecdotal notes

Explanation of the tool and technique: The principal will want to examine the routines used to begin or to come to closure of the class.

How and why this technique is helpful:

This anecdotal technique allows the observer to chronicle activities that support bell-to-bell instruction at two key times during the class period—the beginning and ending of the instructional period. This technique focuses data collection on the events and instructional activities either the beginning or the ending of the period to assess whether time is being used to focus student learning.

Directions and approaches for using the tool: Chronicle the activities and procedures the teacher uses to begin or to end class instruction. Note the amount of time it takes the teacher to open or close class, paying particular attention to the routines, student familiarity with routines, and the cues the teacher uses to signal students.

Tips:

♦ Record data in one- and two-minute increments.

♦ Record major events in detail. A few strong examples with complete and accurate information will make more sense than trying to record extraneous information.

♦ Leave a space such as a large column in the margin to be used during the post-observation conference to make notes (e.g., teacher analysis, questions, concerns, or ideas).

Tool 17 Beginning of Class Observation Form

Teacher: *Amy Kleibar*　　　　Date of observation: *May 6, 2005*

Observer: *Dr. Sou Chen*

Class: *English 7*　　　　　Period of the day: *Period 1*

Time of observation:　　　Start: *8:05*　　End: *8:20*

Total time spent in observation: *15 minutes*

Number of students present: *23*　　Grade level: *9th grade*

Topic of the lesson: *(NA due to focus on beginning of class routines)*

	Beginning of the Period	*Student Behavior*
8:05:	Attendance taken as students enter the room. Teacher in the doorway stopping students as they enter reminding students to take off coats and hats.	Students entering the room and stopping by T's desk to pick up graded papers; students comparing grades as they walk to their desks. (clusters of students clog the doorway and area around T's desk)
8:07:	Bell rings. T closes door and picks up papers left on desk—calls students up to the front of the room to pick up papers.	Students sitting at desk while T gives students their papers; student in row 3 trips a student; two students in row 5 push around books while walking up the aisles.
8:08:	Announcements from the activities office; opens the door for late students; stops at the computer station to log tardy students.	Students sitting at desk: nine students turned around talking to other students during announcements; five students are digging materials out from their book bags; three students lined up at the pencil sharpener.
8:11:	Teacher cues students to review due dates for next essay—points to the board and tells students, "get these dates in notebooks."	Students start opening notebooks...three are trying to borrow paper (no notebooks).

	Beginning of the Period	Student Behavior
8:12:	Teacher cues students, "Review my comments on your papers. Revisions are due tomorrow—rewrite only the parts of the essay circled in green.	Students start thumbing through essays...one student asks what to do if there are no "green circles." Lots of laughter.
8:13:	Teacher cue: "It's a bit noisy in here today...Let's begin by reviewing the elements of an introductory paragraph, but first pull out Writing Tip Sheet 3 from your writing folders...	Students begin looking in book bags for writing folders...several begin to move closer to one another...
8:14:	Teacher offers copies of Writing Tip three to students who do not have this sheet...gives out sheet to 13 students	A student asks, "are we going to finish our group activity from yesterday?"
8:14:	Teacher: First, we're going to review the elements of an introductory paragraph...review silently for a moment the key elements of an introductory paragraph...	Students start to read the sheet.
8:15:	Teacher walks around the room as students read Writing Tip Sheet	Students are quietly reading sheet.
8:18:	Teacher turns on overhead... overhead has a sample introductory paragraph written by the student who had "no green circles" on his paper...teacher cues students to the paragraph and asks them to (1) read the paragraph, (2) compare the elements of an introductory paragraph to the sample on the overhead, and (3) write a few thoughts about the sample paragraph related to the elements found on Tip Sheet 3.	Students focus on the paragraph quietly reading it...many students are writing notes in notebook...a few students are talking with their neighbors...talk is quiet.
8:19–8:20:	Teacher is walking around the room monitoring.	

Tool 18 End of Class Observation Form

Teacher: *Amy Kleibar* Date of observation: *May 6, 2005*

Observer: *Dr. Sou Chen*

Class: *English 7* Period of the day: *Period 1*

Time of observation: Start: *8:45* End: *9:00*

Total time spent in observation: *15 minutes*

Number of students present: *23* Grade level: *9th grade*

Topic of the lesson: *Essay writing*

(NA due to focus on ending of class routines)

		Ending of the Period	Student Behavior
8:45:		Teacher is moving from group to group, speaking with students, examining work...	Students are in small groups discussing essays.
8:48:		Teacher cues students to move desks back in place for large-group processing.	Students start to break out of groups by moving desks back in rows...minimal noise...a student from each group is putting books (thesaurus, dictionary, etc.) back on teacher's desk.
8:49:		Teacher is in front of the room readying for instruction... makes a few statements: (1) Please bring notebooks tomorrow, and I'll add more information about the essay. (2) Also, rewrites on the areas circled in green are due tomorrow, just rewrite the sections circled in green.	Student desks are in a row and students are listening to the teacher, quietly.
8:50:		Let's recap the importance of the advanced organizer in the introductory paragraph and how this organizer serves as a transition to subsequent paragraphs...	Students sit quietly for about 10 seconds...hands start going up...
8:50:		Jamie...	The organizer is the road map and helps the writer point to the major points that get discussed in the essay...in a way it's a writer's compass...

	Ending of the Period	Student Behavior
8:51:	That's an interesting metaphor...a compass...is there any other value to a compass?	Fred responds, the organizer is for the reader, too...the compass helps the traveler know what direction he is in...going...
8:52:	Excellent parallel...let's look at a sample from an essay...teacher flips the overhead on and focuses students to the advanced organizer sentence that is in all bold on the screen...look at this advanced organizer...comment on its importance and value...Lauren...what do you think?	Lauren responds...this organizer has three items in it...the symbols in the book (1) help to illustrate the deeper meaning, (2) provide an understanding of the what motivated the main character, and (3) foreshadow the ending of the book.
8:54:	Superb...now what does the writer need to do next...	Several hands go up...
8:55:	Jackson...what do you think?	"Take time to write another sentence or two...the organizer acts as a segue to the next paragraphs ... Student asks a question, does the advanced organizer have to always have three points?"
8:56:	Actually, the number of points is not important because...	Student responds...it depends on what the essay is trying to get across...
8:56:	That's correct...And we'll be reviewing several more introductory paragraphs tomorrow...let's recap from the day...teacher highlights the Tips for Writing Introductory Paragraphs, the uses and misuses of advanced organizer and the purpose of the advanced organizer.	Students are listening and taking notes...three students are starting to pack up their materials...teacher cues disapproval by standing by the desk of one student...the others stop packing up their materials...
9:00:	Bell rings and teacher thanks the class for working hard and wishes them well for the rest of the day.	Students pack up their bags and start leaving the room.

Cooperative Groups

Background

Cooperative learning is an instructional model in which students complete work as a collaborative learning team in small groups. The work of a cooperative learning group is structured so that each group member contributes to the completion of the learning activity. Cooperative learning group work is sometimes chaotic, with students talking with one another, perhaps even across groups, comparing answers, quizzing one another, or securing materials from bookshelves. In cooperative learning, students assume a variety of active roles including—for example, reader/explainer, checker, and recorder. Within the structure of the cooperative group, the teacher should encourage students to rotate roles to give them opportunities to serve as the reader/explainer, checker, and recorder.

The directions the teacher provides, the monitoring the teacher does within and across groups, and the eye to time on task are essential for cooperative learning to be successful. In cooperative learning, the teacher assumes responsibility for monitoring students' learning and intervening within the groups.

Observation focus: Student interaction, teacher assistance, and monitoring and assessing learning activities

Observation technique: Narrow lens focusing on the work of students in groups and the teacher's monitoring strategies

Explanation of the tool and technique: The cooperative learning model is dependent on small-group work. This tool will assist in tracking not only the work of students but also how a teacher attends to the work of students in small groups.

How and why the technique is helpful: Through monitoring the group activities, the teacher will be able to determine individual student involvement (Johnson & Johnson, 1994). The principal can assist teachers in assessing the work of students, individually or in groups, by collecting data on what students are doing and how students are interacting with one another in cooperative learning groups.

Directions and approaches for using the tool: Once students are in groups, record the interactions of students and the strategies the teacher uses to monitor the work of students within groups.

Tips:
- Track teacher movement from group to group.
- Record teacher verbal cues.

Tool 19 Cooperative Learning

Teacher: *Ms. Theresa Lipinski*　　　Date of Observation: *April 30, 2005*

Observer: *Carol Overman*

Class: *English I*　　　　　　　　Period of the day: *7th period*

Time of observation:　Start: *1:50*　　End: *2:10*

Total time spent in observation: *20 minutes*

Number of students present: *23*　　　Grade level: *Freshman (Honors)*

Topic of the lesson: *Romeo and Juliet*

Group	Number in Group	Student Interaction	Teacher Monitoring Strategies
1	*4*	*Discussing the use of foreshadowing—one student recording comments; one student finding supporting citations from the text; two students talking with one another.*	*Teacher with Group 4*
2	*3*	*Two students reading book, scanning for citations—no talking; one student sketching a crest for the Montague family.*	*Teacher physically with Group 4 but "eye's canning" Group 5 (see notes).*
3	*4*	*One student asking questions—one student writing responses—one student doodling in notebook (Capulet crest)—one student reading book.*	*Teacher moves to Group 5—teacher speaking with group members—full attention to Group 5.*
4	*4*	*Students reading text and alternately speaking with one another...one student starts to draw the family crest for the Capulets.*	*Teacher just moved to Group 5.*

Group	Number in Group	Student Interaction	Teacher Monitoring Strategies
5	4	Two students talking loudly; one student looking in bookbag; one student talking to a student in Group 6.	Teacher "making eye contact" from position in with Group 4...teacher breaks in with an announcement (8 minutes left for group work).
6	4	Two students sharing a book; one student trying to borrow colored pencils for the crest (Capulet); one student reading teacher handout.	Teacher now walking around the room, moving from Group 1 to Group 2... Teacher announces 4 minutes left...asks for a volunteer group to share artistic rendition of the family / royal crest... teacher moves to the front of the room to set up the overhead projector, and CD player...teacher moves back to Group 5...asks for examples of foreshadowing...calls time by asking the question: "How does Shakespeare use foreshadowing from scene 2 forward? ... students start to move desks around to break out of groups...

Depending on when the principal enters the room, a variation on data collection includes using anecdotal notes across the categories that Johnson and Johnson (1994) identified as essential to framing cooperative learning. The following data-collection tool (Tool 20) can help the principal script anecdotal notes while observing in a classroom where cooperative learning is being used.

Tool 20 Alternative Data-Collection Tool
for Tracking Teacher Behaviors Promoting Cooperative Learning

Teacher: *Ms. Janie Adams*   Date of observation: *April 25, 2005*

Observer: *Dr. Brenda Arlin*

Class: *U.S. History*   Period of the day: *2nd period*

Time of observation: Start: *9:05*   End: *9:25*

Total time spent in observation: *20 minutes*

Number of students present: *26*   Grade level: *Juniors*

Topic of the lesson: *Examining how a bill is passed*

Focus on Cooperative Learning	Presence or Absence	Notes
Objectives for the cooperative learning group	X	■ Objective for the activity was written on the whiteboard ■ Teacher referred to the objective as students asked questions. ■ Teacher returned to the objective during closure of group activity.
Clarity of directions	X	■ Before breaking students into groups, teacher gave directions. ■ Teacher distributed directions for each group once students moved into their groups.
Movement into groups	X	■ Six minutes were given for students to move into groups. ■ Materials were bundled for each group in advance of movement.
Monitoring and intervening strategies	X	■ Teacher turned lights on and off to get attention. ■ Teacher broke into group time three times with clarifying directions. ■ Teacher visited each group four times.

Focus on Cooperative Learning	Presence or Absence	Notes
Evaluation strategies		
Interaction with students	X	■ Teacher asked questions and gave feedback to groups while monitoring. ■ Teacher clarified directions. ■ Teacher became a member of each group.
Follow-up instruc-tion—large-group processing	X	■ After 23 minutes, teacher called end to group work. ■ Students moved desks and chairs back in order. ■ Group reporter gave report. ■ Teacher asked and answered questions.

Running Notes with a Timeline

Observation focus: Open-ended, no focus

Observation technique: Anecdotal notes are taken as instruction and classroom activities unfold

Explanation of the tool and technique: The observer writes down as much information as possible, chronicling the activities, instructional methods in use, transition strategies, words of the teacher or of the students, and any other details to provide a broad view of what was observed.

How and why the technique is helpful: Sometimes teachers just want to know generally what was occurring during specific periods of instruction.

Directions and approaches for using the tool: Indicate time and then chronicle what was occurring during the specified time. It is helpful to take notes in five-minute chunks so that the teacher can see patterns during the time in which the notes were taken.

Tips:
- ◆ Record events in 5-minute intervals.
- ◆ Record enough information so that the teacher can make sense of the overall events of the classroom.
- ◆ Include verbal statements as necessary to focus conversation during follow-up with the teacher.
- ◆ Avoid making value judgments while chronicling what is observed.

Tool 21 Running Notes with a Timeline

Teacher: *Mr. Ron Kupinski* Date of observation: *April 28, 2005*

Observer: *Dr. Jesse Cantu*

Class: *2nd grade* Period of the day: *Morning*

Time of observation: Start: *10:00* End: *10:21*

Total time spent in observation: *21 minutes*

Number of students present: *16* Grade level: *2nd Grade*

Topic of the Lesson: *Fractions, Decimals, and Integers*

Time	Running Notes
10:05	■ *Students worked on a problem with the teacher leading students in a quick review of fractions and decimals in every day situations (tax).* ■ *Had students work on a sample problem.*
10:10	■ *Students worked at the their desks—the students who needed additional help put their notebooks on the floor—this is the cue for Mr. Kupinski to go to their desk (about five students clustered in the back put their notebooks on the floor within one minute of starting the sample problem.*
10:14	■ *Mr. Kupinski reviewed skills (quadrants, x and y axis coordinates)* ■ *Showed students how to line coordinates (used an overhead and then showed some computer-generated slides on a PowerPoint)* ■ *Teacher: "Franklin, where is your head at today? Can't you figure this out? (Franklin stops talking but slams pencil down...teacher stops teaching and writes in a notebook).*
10:19	■ *Provided practice with students working on lining up coordinates.*

Looking Ahead...

Now that an informal classroom observation has been conducted, what next? The next step is to be opportunistic and to find time to engage teachers in follow-up conversations. The intent is to foster discussion, reflection, and the momentum to refine practice.

5

Talking with Teachers After Looking In

In This Chapter...

- ◆ Following up after an informal observation
- ◆ Approaches to the post-observation conference
- ◆ Feedback
- ◆ Next steps

You have accomplished quite a bit so far, but conducting informal classroom observations is not enough. The process is not complete without some type of follow-up discussion to the classroom observation, and this time-consuming meeting is why it is important for the principal to develop a manageable schedule of informal classroom observations. It is better to conduct fewer observations each week that include following up with the teacher than to conduct numerous but shorter observations without follow-up discussions. This chapter explores the follow-up process, feedback, and reflection with tips about the next steps that principals can take to enhance their efforts.

Following Up after an Informal Observation

To develop professionally, teachers need opportunities to talk, inquire, and reflect about their practices with the assistance of a colleague. A 20-minute informal observation yields fertile data, and the follow-up process adds value to the observation just conducted. The principal actively demonstrates value for the work teachers do when immediate feedback is provided—both written and, perhaps more profound, through a purposeful discussion in which the meanings of data are explored, with the teacher assuming an active role in the process.

A worst-case scenario is the principal who leaves a note in the teacher's mailbox without any follow-up discussion. The informal observation method that this book promotes includes follow-up discussion but does not preclude written feedback as well. Really, a combination of oral and written feedback is essential to promote ongoing dialogue between the teacher and principal. Tool 22 details a written feedback form that is helpful to use as a prompt for follow-up discussion. Effective principals balance written and oral feedback. Some principals find it helpful to give written feedback immediately after the observation and then to follow up with discussion. By giving written feedback prior to the follow-up discussion, the teacher has time to absorb the information. However, some principals may find it useful to bring the written feedback to the post-observation conference. Time and circumstances will dictate which approach the principal takes.

Tool 22 Sample Informal Post-Observation Feedback Form

Teacher: *Dr. Patty Braveman*   Date of observation: *May 23, 2005*

Observer: *Jennifer Spinks*   Class: *Spanish I*

Period of the day: *2nd period*

Time of observation: Start: *9:30*   End: *9:50*

Total time spent in observation: *20 minutes*

Number of students present: *18*

Grade level: *Mixed Freshman, Sophomore, Junior*

Topic of the Lesson: *How to tell time in Spanish*

Students were

- ☑ working in small, cooperative groups
- ☐ making a presentation
- ☐ taking a test
- ☒ working independently at their desks
- ☐ viewing a film
- ☐ other: Pair-share groups to practice telling time in Spanish

Teacher was

- ☒ lecturing
- ☐ facilitating a question and answer sequence
- ☐ working independently with students
- ☒ demonstrating a concept
- ☒ introducing a new concept
- ☐ reviewing for a test
- ☐ coming to closure
- ☐ other _____

Comments:

Patty: Wow and more Wow on your efforts to provide solid instruction and to engage a group of students in the lesson on how to tell time in Spanish. The introduction hooked students because you: (1) used prompts (e.g., the big clock, smaller clocks for each student and their groups), (2) incorporated the use of time with prior lesson content (e.g., ordering a meal, asking for directions, making a long distance call in a different time zone), and (3) kept the small pair-share groups focused with written directions on the oral exercise to practice before getting back into large group.

Students were eagerly ready to share once the "round robin" "time talk" began after your introductory lecture and the pair-share groups finished. The hands that "flew up" signaled that students were eager to show you what they had learned.

For our discussion later today, I am interested on how you gauge wait time in a foreign language.

I look forward to our meeting.

Jennifer Spinks

Post-Observation Conferences

The intent of the post-observation conference is for the teacher and principal to

- review and analyze the data collected
- reflect on meanings
- examine future possibilities for ongoing professional development and refinement of practice

First and foremost, effective post-observation conferences are

- time bound
- place bound
- dialogue bound

Post-Observation Conferences Are Time Bound

Time is important; if too much time elapses between the observation and the conference, the data lose meaning, and teachers lose motivation to learn from the process of using data to reconstruct the events of the class observation. Timely feedback occurs within 48 hours of the observation. Some principals meet with teachers immediately after the observation. To do this, the principal must plan a follow-up conversation with the teacher during a preparation period, meet with the teacher over lunch, or find a substitute for a portion of the teacher's duty period to facilitate conversation. As a principal, you are encouraged to become opportunistic and creative in finding time during the day to meet with teachers. Find time before, after, and during the day for follow-up opportunities.

Post-Observation Conferences Are Place Bound

The place where follow-up occurs is significant. Holding the post-observation conference in the principal's office puts the principal in a position of authority. Conducting the post-observation conference in the classroom where the observation occurred helps to recreate the context of the learning environment. It also offers the teacher and principal appropriate and immediate props to demonstrate the points made in observation. Atmosphere is essential; the post-observation conference opens the door to future dialogue and growth. However, the library, media center, faculty lounge, and other accessible areas of the school provide appropriate places for the principal and teacher to meet. Although privacy is essential, public places should not be avoided. The principal who is out and about is visible talking with teachers between classes, during duty periods, at the bus stop, at sporting events—any place where teachers are.

Post-Observation Conferences Are Dialogue Bound

McGreal (1983) asserted that the more teachers talk about teaching, the better they get at it. Post-observation conferences should invite ongoing dialogue between the teacher and principal. Although written follow-up is acceptable, effort should be made to engage teachers in discussion and reflection. Not only do teachers have an opportunity to talk about their teaching and analyze data during follow-up, but they also have the opportunity to

- reflect on practice
- express concerns
- pinpoint areas they want to pursue further with formal and informal professional development

Lesson Reconstruction

One method, *lesson reconstruction* (Bellon & Bellon, 1982), elevates the teacher as an integral part of the active learning process, engaged as a learner in the process of deriving meaning from the analysis of data collected during classroom observation. The lesson-reconstruction method calls for follow up the same day, if possible. In this method, the teacher and the principal use the data to reconstruct the events of the classroom. One strategy to assist with lesson reconstruction is to leave the notes from the observation with the teacher while exiting the classroom (see Tool 23). Included with the raw observation notes should be the time and place of the post-observation conference to ensure that this important aspect of the informal observation does not get put on the "back burner" because of distraction caused by other responsibilities.

Tool 23 Presentation of Post-Observation Conference Notes

Teacher: *Mr. Ron Kupinski*   Date of observation: *April 28, 2005*

Observer: *Dr. Jesse Cantu*

Class: *Grade 2*   Period of the day: *Morning*

Time of observation: Start: *10:00*   End: *10:21*

Total time spent in observation: *21 minutes*

Number of students present: *16*   Grade level: *3rd grade*

Topic of the lesson: *Fractions, Decimals, and Integers*

Post-observation conference date and location:
April 3, 2005—3rd Period (Ron, I have a sub for your assigned duty period. Let's meet in your classroom, Jesse.)

Time	Running Notes	Teacher Questions
10:05	■ Students worked on a problem with the teacher leading students in a quick review of fractions and decimals in every day situations (tax).	Was my review too brisk given the observation that five students needed help within 1 minute of starting independent practice?
10:10	■ Had students work on a sample problem. ■ Students worked at the their desks—the students who needed additional help put their notebooks on the floor—this is the cue for Mr. Kupinski to go to their desk (about five students clustered in the back put their notebooks on the floor within one minute of starting the sample problem.	

Time	Running Notes	Teacher Questions
10:14	■ Mr. Kupinski reviewed skills (quadrants, x and y axis coordinates) ■ Showed students how to line coordinates (used an overhead and then showed some computer-generated slides on a PowerPoint) ■ Teacher: "Franklin, where is your head at today? Can't you figure this out? (Franklin stops talking but slams pencil down...teacher stops teaching and writes in a notebook.)	I can't get a sense of how often to review—I think they get it and then, wham, I lose two or three students. I'm thinking about appealing more to multiple intelligences...but I use overheads and other technology. Any ideas? I need help with Franklin—today he was mild.
10:19	■ Provided practice with students working on lining up coordinates.	

If the principal leaves these notes with the teacher, the teacher will need to take time to reflect on the data and pose questions based on the observation notes. During the follow-up discussion, the teacher and principal review the notes and the corresponding questions the teacher has written on the form. From there, the teacher and principal engage in a discussion of the data. Although spontaneity is encouraged, the events chronicled by the principal frame the discussion. The following questions are useful in guiding the discussion:

◆ How do you think the lesson went?
◆ What went well?
◆ What would you do again if you were teaching this same lesson?
◆ What would you do differently?
◆ Overall, how do you think this lesson went in comparison to the same lesson taught with a different group of students?

Again, the data and the teacher's insights will frame the discussion. This technique points to the importance of the principal's ability to chronicle data during the classroom observation.

Effective Principals Are Prepared

Being prepared for discussion during follow-up with the teacher is essential; principals make judgment calls on whether follow-up should be done in writing, orally through a discussion with the teacher, or a combination of both. Planning time gives the principal the opportunity to organize the raw data gathered during the observation. Teaching is fast paced, and the principal records observations at an equally fast pace. In its final form, the data must be clear and understandable to both the teacher and the principal. To lay the groundwork for a successful post-observation conference, the principal tackles several tasks:

- *Revisit the focus of the classroom observation.* Reviewing the data, the principal looks for direct or striking examples of classroom practices that relate specifically to the focus. One approach is to identify events that contributed to achieving an objective or prevented the teacher from achieving an objective.

- *Develop a strategy for presenting the data collected during the observation.* Providing the teacher with objective feedback is dependent on displaying the data clearly and the ability to return to the data for clarification, explanation, or extension during the post-observation conference. The observer's role is to facilitate the teacher's self-analysis and reflection based on the data. The conference plan should keep the teacher reflecting on and analyzing the events of the classroom.

- *Frame an opening to get the teacher thinking and talking about teaching.* Effective invitations to dialogue, also called "icebreakers," are open-ended statements related to some aspect of teaching. Figure 5.1 presents examples of icebreaker and conversation-stopper statements.

Figure 5.1 Comparison of Post-Observation Icebreaker Statements

Icebreaker Statements	*Conversation Stoppers*
Think back to [some aspect of the lesson or the class] and tell me about it.	Prove to me that the students were prepared for independent practice.
The approach you chose to break students into small groups helped students learn how to cooperate. Tell me how you were able to get students to this level of cooperation.	No matter what you say, I just can't believe that the students will be ready to work in cooperative groups.
Tell me more about [some aspect of the class, student response, an instructional method, and predictions about how students will perform on an assessment].	I'd like for you to turn in the results of your next quiz. I saw too many students struggling with their work during independent practice. Don't you think that more guided practice would have been more appropriate?
When you looked at Johnny, he knew immediately to stop talking. How did you know how and when to look at him like this? Is Johnny the only student who responds to your look to stop talking? How did you know to use that look?	Don't get too confident about Johnny, he'll talk while you are working with other students.
For the students who were absent the day before, you used activity time to help them catch up. What about the students in the activity? Can the students catch up another way?	Just analyze my notes and then get back to me if you have any questions about my assessment of your teaching.
How did you know that the student would try to…	Stop babying these kids; they are about to graduate and need to be more self-sufficient, don't you agree?

Approaches to the Post-Observation Conference

To make the follow-up discussion more inviting and meaningful, a facilitative style, in which the principal is open to hearing what the teacher has to say, will be most helpful to the teacher. Remember, the follow-up discussion is about the teacher, not the principal. The teacher's point of view must permeate the discussion. Talking about teaching is a cooperative endeavor. It is the principal's duty to engage the teacher in reviewing, analyzing, and reflecting on data. Through effort, patience, and willingness to be of assistance, principals can help teachers make progress in their professional development. To establish a cooperative learning experience for the teacher, the supervisor's style and approach to communication must promote teacher talk. Figure 5.2 identifies ways to promote teacher dialogue, inquiry, and reflection.

Figure 5.2 Approaches to Promoting Dialogue, Inquiry, and Reflection

Approach	*Example*
Remain objective by providing the teacher with observational data that is value-free and nonjudgmental.	Here are the events that led to the small group…
Listen more—talk less—in order to hear (understand) what the teacher is trying to communicate.	Examine the following notes and tell me what responses you anticipated from students after you asked for…
Acknowledge, paraphrase, and ask probing and clarifying questions that encourage the teacher to talk more. Open-ended questions help the teacher make discoveries, identify recurring patterns, and reflect on possible alternatives or extensions to instructional practices.	From your point of view, what made this lesson successful? At what point did you sense the students were "getting it"?
Encourage the teacher to expand on statements that share beliefs about teaching, learning, and students.	When the student in the red shirt said, "This is stupid," what made it possible for you to continue with the activity?
State what went well and ask reflective questions to focus on what needs improvement from the teacher's point of view.	The small group activity really worked well. How do you think the transition back to large group could have been different?
Avoid giving directive types of advice—even if asked. Instead, engage the teacher in role playing reprises of events you observed, then invite extended thinking. Role playing and simulations that reflect the teacher's practices are more realistic.	Let me pretend I am a student in your fourth hour class. How would you help me understand the concepts important to today's unit discussion?

Approach	Example
Refuse to engage in talk not related to what you directly observed or to the improvement of instruction.	That thought is important. After the post-observation conference, I'll share your idea with the assistant principal.
Offer to return for further observations in order to keep the momentum going for the teacher.	When would be a good time for me to come back to see the students apply the formula?
Provide ongoing support for the decisions the teacher makes in the post-observation conference by investigating with the teacher follow-up learning or enrichment activities.	The district is offering an after-school workshop on higher order thinking. Perhaps you'd like to go. I'll make a reservation for you.
Be aware of nonverbal behavior that can send mixed messages. Convey interest and concern.	Looking at the clock, facial expressions, and body language such as folded arms.

Feedback

Teachers need and want to know how they are doing and what they can do to improve or modify an approach; moreover, teachers need to be affirmed for their efforts. Data should be the only source of feedback, and the principal should take care not to impose bias or judgment on observation data. Framing and giving feedback are complicated. People want praise for their efforts, but they also want honesty in knowing when their efforts might need adjustment. It is often easier to give positive rather than negative feedback. Providing both types of feedback will require tact, wise word choice, and clear communication. Principals cannot afford any hidden messages in their words. Hidden messages can enhance or block the future efforts of the principal and teacher.

Types of Feedback

Feedback can be confirmatory or corrective, according to Kurtoglu-Hooton (2004) who details the work of Egan (2002). Based on the preliminary research of Kurtoglu-Hooton (pp. 1–3), confirmatory feedback is

- given in the context of praise in connection with what the teacher did well

- likely to encourage a teacher to construct his/her own constructive thought patterns and may encourage teachers to try new avenues and to pursue new challenges

Conversely, corrective feedback is
- based on expected behaviors
- applied to situations where there may have been a better course of action (behavior), such as the need to show an awareness of learner errors and being able to correct them sensitively or ensuring there is a purpose for using an activity
- based on "a gentle telling off" if the teacher seems to be repeating the same mistakes without any evidence of moving forward. Corrective feedback requires a period of time for the teacher to process, digest, reflect upon and come to terms with the "criticism" involved.

Kurtoglu-Hooton (2004) also asserted that confirmatory feedback is often less detailed than corrective feedback, and that "if it is supported with specific examples from the teacher's lesson, there is every reason that this type of feedback, too, would facilitate teacher change. Teacher learning and change do not have to be problem-oriented all the time" (p. 4).

Feedback can be constructive or destructive. Consider the following statements:

1. "Mrs. Ritter, you really need to take the workshop. All the questions you asked were lower-level ones. Students were obviously bored with your inability to ask for more than recall of information."

2. "Mrs. Ritter, your insight about your questions asking students for recall reminds me of how I used to ask opening questions. I benefited from the county workshop *Questioning Strategies that Promote Higher-Order Thinking*. This session is on the schedule for next month; would you be interested in attending? We have the funds and with advance notice, I can lock in a sub for you."

Statement 1 is destructive; it is too blunt, and it puts the teacher down with a personal attack. Statement 2 communicates the same message—the teacher needs assistance with questioning strategies—but in a more proactive way.

Proactive feedback provides objective insight based on data without criticizing the teacher or finding fault. This type of feedback promotes a willingness to take risks and to be more open to changing practice. Destructive feedback, by contrast, attacks aspects that are beyond control (such as the sound of the teacher's voice) or belittles teachers by compiling data that point only to weaknesses. Figure 5.3 lists characteristics of effective feedback.

Figure 5.3 Characteristics of Effective Feedback

Effective feedback in the post-observation conference does the following:

- supports the teacher in examining both the positive and the not-so-positive aspects of practice
- promotes footholds for follow-up
- nurtures a sense of worth and positive self-esteem
- facilitates self-assessment and self-discovery
- Focuses on a few key areas
- describes accurately what was observed
- is authentic and free of meaningless or patronizing platitudes
- clarifies and expands ideas for both the teacher and the observer
- deals with the concrete examples observed (actions, behaviors, words of the teacher or students)
- promotes goal setting and the development of strategies
- avoids
  - making assumptions about teachers
  - overloading the teacher with detail after detail after detail
  - evaluating the teacher's overall credibility as a teacher
  - asserting or making inferences about the teacher
  - judging and labeling a practice as good or bad
- guides the teacher to think beyond the lesson observed
- accepts and incorporates the points the teacher makes as part of the feedback process

Data Overload

In an attempt to be helpful, some principals fall into the trap of overwhelming the teacher with too much information. Principals who attempt to establish their credibility may fall into the trap of offering a laundry list of observations based on their view of the lesson. But supervision is not about the principal; supervision is about the teacher and the learning opportunity that the data and feedback from an observation can provide. The tenor of the feedback in the post-observation conference sets the tone for future interaction between the principal and the teacher. However, even carefully framed feedback may not be well received. The way a teacher receives feedback depends on variables such as the degree of trust between the supervisor and teacher, the experience level of the teacher, the patterns of communication at the school, and the conditions surrounding the classroom observation.

Feedback is effective because of its frequency, timing, specificity, and contextualized nature.

- *Frequency:* Feedback should be given often (this means that principals need to get supervision "out of the main office").
- *Timing:* Feedback should be given as soon as humanly possible after a formal or informal observation. Time fades the memory. Think of the difficulties in recreating the events of the classroom even with stable data collected during an observation.
- *Specificity:* With stable data, feedback should be related to specific events as they unfolded in the classroom.
- *Contextualized nature:* Feedback must be given based classroom variables such as the characteristics of students, the experience level of the teacher, and the focus of the classroom observation.

Feedback is critical to any instructional supervisory model. Without feedback after a classroom observation, it is unlikely that growth and development will occur or that teachers will make changes in their classroom practices.

Next Steps

The follow-up process extends beyond the feedback and links informal classroom observations to professional development. Through a series of informal classroom observations with written and verbal feedback, both the teacher and the principal are aware of areas to focus on. To promote professional development, the teacher and principal should consider the following activities:

- attend workshops, seminars, and conferences
- observe another teacher in the building or district
- enroll in a graduate course
- engage in action research with a common grade or subject area teacher
- form a study group after identifying a topic of interest (e.g., differentiated instructional practices for gifted and talented students), read a book or a series of articles related to the topic of interest, and then meet as a group to discuss ideas and strategies gleaned from the readings. Follow-up could include moving ideas into an action research project or pairing up to observe others who share the desire to implement a new strategy.
- develop or refine a portfolio

The possibilities are endless. Follow-up holds great promise as a supervisory tool. During this time, teachers have the opportunity to analyze and make sense of data that bring some aspect of their teaching into focus. Lesson reconstruction as advocated by Bellon and Bellon (1982) engages the teacher in rebuilding the events of the classroom using data to analyze effectiveness. When the principal offers objective feedback, the teacher is in a better position to make informed judgments about practice and to develop further plans for growth and change.

Looking Ahead...

The tools used throughout this book are presented in the Appendix. The tools are blank so that the busy principal can reproduce them to collect data during informal classroom observations.

Appendix

Classroom Observation Tools

Throughout each chapter, tools to assist the principal frame and conduct classroom observations are offered. Each tool presented in the chapters is provided as a blank form in this Appendix to help the busy principal collect useable and stable data during informal classroom observations.[1]

---

1 Unless indicated, all tools are from Zepeda (2003). Used with permission.

Tool 1 Assessing the Broad Characteristics of a Faculty

1. Number of teachers = _____   Male = _____ Female = _____

2. For each teacher, tally the number of years in teaching.
   Total number of years of experience = _____
   Average years of faculty experience = _____

3. Number of teachers whose experience falls within the following service ranges:

   a. 1–3 years = _____

   b. 4–7 years = _____

   c. 8–11 years = _____

   d. 12–15 years = _____

   e. 16–19 years = _____

   f. 20+ years = _____

4. Number of first-year teachers = _____
   Number of teachers who will retire at the end of the year = _____

5. Wildcards:
   First-year teachers with experience = _____
   Alternatively certified teachers = _____
   Teachers returning to work after an extended leave = _____
   Other = _____

6. What overall patterns do you notice?

Tool 2 Tracking Informal Observations

Teacher	Observer	Informal Observations	Date of Follow-up	Formal Observations	Period(s)/ Time(s)	Follow-up Topics

Tool 3 Selective Verbatim[2]

Teacher: _____ Date of observation: _____

Class: _____ Period of the day: _____

Observer: _____

Time of observation: Start: _____ End: _____

Total time spent in observation: _____

Number of students present: _____ Grade level: _____

Topic of the lesson: _____

Teacher Comment/ Response	Time	Praise	Correction	Preventive Prompt
Ratio of praise to correction:				
Preventive prompts:				

---

2 Developed by Theresa L. Benfante, Behavior Interventionist at Central Alternative School, Cobb County School District (Georgia). Used with permission.

Tool 4 Checklist Classroom Observation Form

Teacher: _____ Date of observation: _____

Class: _____ Period of the day: _____

Observer: _____

Time of observation: Start: _____End: _____

Total time spent in observation: _____

Number of students present: _____ Grade level: _____

Topic of the lesson: _____

Students were

☐ working in small, cooperative groups

☐ making a presentation

☐ taking a test

☐ working independently at their desks

☐ viewing a film

☐ other _____

Teacher was

☐ lecturing

☐ facilitating a question and answer sequence

☐ working independently with students

☐ demonstrating a concept

☐ introducing a new concept

☐ reviewing for a test

☐ coming to closure

☐ other _____

Comments:

Tool 5 Anecdotal and Checklist Data Collection Method, Focus on Cooperative Learning

Teacher: _____ Date of observation: _____

Class: _____ Period of the day: _____

Observer: _____

Time of observation: Start: _____End: _____

Total time spent in observation: _____

Number of students present: _____ Grade level: _____

Topic of the lesson: _____

Focus on Cooperative Learning	*Presence or Absence*	*Notes*
Objectives for the cooperative learning group		
Clarity of directions		
Movement into groups		
Monitoring and intervening strategies		
Evaluation strategies		
Interaction with students		
Follow-up instruction—large-group processing		

Tool 6 Foreign Language Observation Checklist[3]

Teacher: _____ Date of observation: _____

Class: _____ Period of the day: _____

Observer: _____

Time of observation: Start: _____ End: _____

Total time spent in observation: _____

Number of students present: _____ Grade level: _____

Topic of the lesson: _____

A successful foreign language classroom should provide the following:

1. Are all language modalities evident in the lesson (speaking, writing, listening, and reading) as well as culture?

2. Does the teacher use a wide variety of prepared and authentic materials at appropriate levels?

3. Is the purpose of each activity clearly explained to the students?

4. Does the teacher model activities when giving directions and check for comprehension afterwards?

5. Are the transitions between activities smooth?

6. Are the students on task and actively involved in the learning process?

7. Is there an appropriate use of partner–pair or small group activities?

8. Does the classroom have a nurturing, nonthreatening atmosphere where mutual respect is clearly demonstrated?

Other?

Comments: _____

---

3 Developed by Marcia Wilbur, Ph.D., and Head of World Languages and Cultures Professional Development at The College Board, based on her work at Gull Lake High School Foreign Language Department, Richland, Michigan. Used with permission.

Tool 7 Seating Chart Data Collection Tool

Teacher: _____ Date of observation: _____

Class: _____ Period of the day: _____

Observer: _____

Time of observation: Start: _____End: _____

Total time spent in observation: _____

Number of students present: _____ Grade level: _____

Topic of the lesson: _____

Comments:

Tool 8: Observation Guide Using Bloom's Taxonomy

Teacher: _____ Date of observation: _____

Class: _____ Period of the day: _____

Observer: _____

Time of observation: Start: _____End: _____

Total time spent in observation: _____

Number of students present: _____ Grade level: _____

Topic of the lesson: _____

| | | Levels of Thinking | | | | | |
Time	Questions	K N O W L E D G E	C O M P R E H E N S I O N	A P P L I C A T I O N	A N A L Y S I S	S Y N T H E S I S	E V A L U A T I O N

Tool 9 Alternate Observation Guide Using Bloom's Taxonomy

Teacher: _____ Date of observation: _____

Class: _____ Period of the day: _____

Observer: _____

Time of observation: Start: _____End: _____

Total time spent in observation: _____

Number of students present: _____ Grade level: _____

Topic of the lesson: _____

Time	Teacher Questions	Taxonomy Level

Tool 10 Focus on Wait Time

Teacher: _____ Date of observation: _____

Class: _____ Period of the day: _____

Observer: _____

Time of observation: Start: _____End: _____

Total time spent in observation: _____

Number of students present: _____ Grade level: _____

Topic of the lesson: _____

Teacher Question	*Wait Time (seconds)*

Tool 11 Wait Time Combined with Bloom's Taxonomy for Examining Levels of Questions

Teacher: _____ Date of observation: _____

Class: _____ Period of the day: _____

Observer: _____

Time of observation: Start: _____End: _____

Total time spent in observation: _____

Number of students present: _____ Grade level: _____

Topic of the lesson: _____

Teacher Question	Wait Time (seconds)	Question Domain

Tool 12 Cause and Effect

Teacher: _____ Date of observation: _____

Class: _____ Period of the day: _____

Observer: _____

Time of observation: Start: _____End: _____

Total time spent in observation: _____

Number of students present: _____ Grade level: _____

Topic of the lesson: _____

Teacher Behavior	*Student Response or Activity*

Tool 13 Variety of Instructional Methods

Teacher: _____ Date of observation: _____

Class: _____ Period of the day: _____

Observer: _____

Time of observation: Start: _____End: _____

Total time spent in observation: _____

Number of students present: _____ Grade level: _____

Topic of the lesson: _____

Time	Instructional Method	Teacher Behavior	Student Activities

Tool 14 Examining Teacher–Student Discussion with a Focus on How Student Comments Are Incorporated into the Lesson

Teacher: _____ Date of observation: _____

Class: _____ Period of the day: _____

Observer: _____

Time of observation: Start: _____ End: _____

Total time spent in observation: _____

Number of students present: _____ Grade level: _____

Topic of the lesson: _____

Time	Teacher Talk/ Question	Student Response	How Student Comments are Used

Tool 15 Focus on Tracking Transition Patterns

Teacher: _____ Date of observation: _____

Class: _____ Period of the day: _____

Observer: _____

Time of observation: Start: _____ End: _____

Total time spent in observation: _____

Number of students present: _____ Grade level: _____

Topic of the lesson: _____

Instruction/Activity	Transition	Student Response

Tool 16 Tracking Student Behavior

Teacher: _____ Date of observation: _____

Class: _____ Period of the day: _____

Observer: _____

Time of observation: Start: _____End: _____

Total time spent in observation: _____

Number of students present: _____ Grade level: _____

Topic of the lesson: _____

Teacher	&	Student

Tool 17 Beginning Class Observation Form

Teacher: _____ Date of observation: _____

Class: _____ Period of the day: _____

Observer: _____

Time of observation: Start: _____End: _____

Total time spent in observation: _____

Number of students present: _____ Grade level: _____

Topic of the lesson: _____

Beginning of the Period	*Student Behavior*

Tool 18 End of Class Observation Form

Teacher: _____ Date of observation: _____

Class: _____ Period of the day: _____

Observer: _____

Time of observation: Start: _____End: _____

Total time spent in observation: _____

Number of students present: _____ Grade level: _____

Topic of the lesson: _____

Ending of the Period	*Student Behavior*

Tool 19 Cooperative Groups

Teacher: _____ Date of observation: _____

Class: _____ Period of the day: _____

Observer: _____

Time of observation: Start: _____End: _____

Total time spent in observation: _____

Number of students present: _____ Grade level: _____

Topic of the lesson: _____

Group	Number in Group	Student Interaction	Teacher Monitoring Strategies
1			
2			
3			
4			
5			
6			
7			

Tool 20 Alternate Data-Collection Tool for Tracking Teacher Behaviors Promoting Cooperative Learning

Teacher: _____ Date of observation: _____

Class: _____ Period of the day: _____

Observer: _____

Time of observation: Start: _____End: _____

Total time spent in observation: _____

Number of students present: _____ Grade level: _____

Topic of the lesson: _____

Focus on Cooperative Learning	Presence or Absence	Notes
Objectives for the cooperative learning group		
Clarity of directions		
Monitoring and intervening strategies		
Principles of Cooperative Learning	Presence or Absence	Notes
Evaluation strategies		
Interactions with students		
Follow-up instruction		

Tool 21 Running Notes with a Timeline

Teacher: _____ Date of observation: _____

Class: _____ Period of the day: _____

Observer: _____

Time of observation: Start: _____End: _____

Total time spent in observation: _____

Number of students present: _____ Grade level: _____

Topic of the lesson: _____

Time	Running Notes

Tool 22 Sample Informal Post-Observation Feedback Form

Teacher: _____ Date of observation: _____

Class: _____ Period of the day: _____

Observer: _____

Time of observation: Start: _____End: _____

Total time spent in observation: _____

Number of students present: _____ Grade level: _____

Topic of the lesson: _____

Students were

- ☐ working in small, cooperative groups
- ☐ making a presentation
- ☐ taking a test
- ☐ working independently at their desks
- ☐ viewing a film
- ☐ other _____

Teacher was

- ☐ lecturing
- ☐ facilitating a question and answer sequence
- ☐ working independently with students
- ☐ demonstrating a concept
- ☐ introducing a new concept
- ☐ reviewing for a test
- ☐ coming to closure
- ☐ other _____

Comments:

Tool 23 Presentation of Post-Observation Conference Notes

Teacher: _____ Date of observation: _____

Class: _____ Period of the day: _____

Observer: _____

Time of observation: Start: _____End: _____

Total time spent in observation: _____

Number of students present: _____ Grade level: _____

Topic of the lesson: _____

Post-observation conference date and location: _____

Time	Running Notes	Teacher Questions

References

Acheson, K. A., & Gall, M. D. (1997). *Techniques in the clinical supervision of teachers: Preservice and inservice applications* (4th ed.). White Plains, NY: Longman.

Bellon, J. J., & Bellon, E. C. (1982). *Classroom supervision and instructional improvement: A synergetic process* (2nd ed.). Dubuque, IA: Kendall/Hunt.

Blase, J. R., & Blase, J. J. (1998). *Handbook of instructional leadership: How really good principals promote teaching and learning.* Thousand Oaks, CA: Corwin.

Bloom, B. S. (Ed.). (1956). *Taxonomy of educational objectives: The classification of educational goals.* New York: Longman.

Brookfield, S. D. (1986). *Understanding and facilitating adult learning: A comprehensive analysis of principles and effective practices.* San Francisco: Jossey-Bass.

Burden, P. (1982, February). *Developmental supervision: Reducing teacher stress at different career stages.* Paper presented at the Association of Teacher Educators National Conference, Phoenix, AZ.

Burke, P. J., Christensen, J. C., & Fessler, R. (1984). *Teacher career stages: Implications for staff development.* Bloomington, IN: Phi Delta Kappa Educational Foundation.

Christensen, J. P., Burke, P. J., Fessler, R., & Hagstrom, D. (1983). *Stages of teachers' careers: Implications for professional development.* Washington, DC: National Institute of Education. (ERIC Document Reproduction Service No. ED227054)

Downey, C. J., Steffy, B. E., English, F. W., Frase, L. E., & Poston, W. K., Jr. (2004). *Changing school supervisory practices one teacher at a time: The three-minute classroom walk-through.* Thousand Oaks, CA: Corwin.

Feiman, S., & Floden, R. (1980). *What's all this talk about teacher development?* East Lansing, MI: Institute for Research on Teaching. (ERIC Document Reproduction Service No. ED189088)

FutureCents. (n.d.). *Twelve guidelines for managing by walking around (MBWA).* Retrieved February 14, 2005, from www.futruecents.com/mainmbwa.htm.

Huberman, M. (1993). *The lives of teachers* (Jonathan Neufeld, Trans.). New York: Teachers College Press.

Johnson, D. W., & Johnson, R. T. (1994). Learning together. In S. Sharan (Ed.), *Handbook of cooperative learning methods* (pp. 51–65). Westport, CT: Greenwood Press.

Katz, L. (1972). Developmental stages of preschool teachers. *Elementary School Journal, 73*(1), 50–54.

Knowles, M. S. (1980). *The modern practice of adult education: From pedagogy to andragogy* (2nd ed.). Chicago: Follett.

Kurtoglu-Hooton, N. (2004, July). Post-observation feedback as an instigator of teacher learning and change. *International Association of Teachers of English as a Foreign Language TTED SIG E-Newsletter.* Retrieved February 28, 2005, from www.ihes.com/ttsig/resources/e-newsletter/FreatureArticles.pdf.

Manning, R. C. (1988). *The teacher evaluation handbook: Step-by-step techniques and forms for improving instruction.* Paramus, NJ: Prentice Hall.

McGreal, T. L. (1983). *Effective teacher evaluation.* Alexandria, VA: Association for Supervision and Curriculum Development.

McGreal, T. L. (1988). Evaluation for enhancing instruction: Linking teacher evaluation and staff development. In S. J. Stanley & W. J. Popham (Eds.), *Teacher evaluation: Six prescriptions for success* (pp. 1–29). Alexandria, VA: Association for Supervision and Curriculum Development.

Peters, T. J., & Waterman, R. H., Jr. (1982). *In search of excellence: Lessons from America's best run companies.* New York: Harper & Row.

Rowe, M. B. (1986). Wait time: Slowing down may be a way of speeding up. *Journal of Teacher Education, 37*(1), 43–50.

Stahl, R. J. (1994). *Using "think-time" and "wait-time" skillfully in the classroom.* Bloomington, IN: ERIC Clearinghouse for Social Studies/Social Science Education. Retrieved February 25, 2005, from http://atozteacherstuff.com/pages/1884.shtml.

Tomlinson, C. A. (1999). *The differentiated classroom: Responding to the needs of all learners.* Alexandria, VA: Association for Supervision and Curriculum Development.

Zepeda. S. J. (2003). *The principal as instructional leader: A handbook for supervisors.* Larchmont, NY: Eye on Education.